ALL THE WAY
BY THE
GRAND CANAL

First published 2023 by The O'Brien Press Ltd.,
12 Terenure Road East, Rathgar, Dublin 6, D06 HD27, Ireland.
Tel: +353 1 4923333; Fax: +353 1 4922777
E-mail: books@obrien.ie. Website: obrien.ie
The O'Brien Press is a member of Publishing Ireland.

ISBN: 978-1-78849-343-7

10 9 8 7 6 5 4 3 2 1
27 26 25 24 23

Photography by Richard Mills

Printed and bound in Poland by Bialostockie Zaklady Graficzne S.A.
The paper in this book is produced using pulp from managed forests.

Published in

ALL THE WAY
— BY THE —
GRAND CANAL

JO KERRIGAN & RICHARD MILLS

Jo Kerrigan & Richard Mills

THE O'BRIEN PRESS
DUBLIN

JO KERRIGAN was born and bred in Cork, where she took her first two degrees at UCC before moving to the UK to continue her academic work. After a distinguished career there, including winning the Oxbow Prize for medieval history at Oxford, she returned to her roots to apply her research skills to Ireland's undiscovered past. A specialist in ancient crafts and folklore, she now devotes herself to exploring how everyday life was lived long ago.

RICHARD MILLS was born in Provence, and moved to Ireland at the age of sixteen. His long and successful career as a press photographer was combined with a passion for wildlife, and his pictures have garnered numerous national and international awards. He was the subject of a TV programme by the wildlife film-maker Éamon de Buitléar, and he has contributed images to hundreds of publications across the world, as well as his own popular book, *Ireland's Bird Life: A World of Beauty*.

Jo and Richard live in West Cork, surrounded by books and cameras, cats and dogs. Previous books for O'Brien Press include *West Cork: A Place Apart*, *Old Ways, Old Secrets*, *Follow the Old Road*, *Brehon Laws*, and *Stories From the Sea*.

Dedicated to
the un-named, unacknowledged, thousands
who laboriously dug that great waterway
from the Liffey to the Shannon
and bequeathed to us such a great heritage.

TABLE
OF
CONTENTS

	INTRODUCTION	page 9
	A BRIEF HISTORY OF THE CANAL	17
Ch I	ALL AROUND THE CITY	23
Ch II	GRIFFITH BRIDGE TO LUCAN	43
Ch III	LUCAN TO SALLINS	61
Ch IV	SALLINS TO ROBERTSTOWN	77
Ch V	THE BARROW LINE: LOWTOWN TO ATHY	93
Ch VI	ROBERTSTOWN TO EDENDERRY	119
Ch VII	EDENDERRY TO TULLAMORE	137
Ch VIII	TULLAMORE TO TURRAUN	157
Ch IX	TURRAUN TO SHANNON HARBOUR	171
	INDEX OF PLACES	190

Kilbeggan

Ballinasloe

The Grand Canal

Dublin

Shannon Harbour

Mountmellick

Naas

Athy

River Shannon

River Barrow

INTRODUCTION

Ireland's Grand Canal is both an incredible inheritance and a priceless asset in our lives today. A long-distance walking and cycling way (132km, 82 miles), it stretches right across Ireland, connecting the capital city, Dublin, on the east coast, with the mighty Shannon and open access to the Atlantic on the west coast. It is there for all of us, at all seasons, either to stroll in sections as the mood takes us, or, for an adventurous challenge, to travel its entire length. Start at one end or the other, drop in to the towpath that is nearest to your home, or treat it as Ireland's own *camino*, and walk it slowly, savouring its scenery, its wildlife, and its history.

Because, when you travel along the Grand Canal, you are travelling through history itself, past quiet countryside that saw mighty construction works, miracles of architecture, ever-moving camps of workers. Everywhere along these banks individuals and households depended on its traffic: the barges, the goods, the people on them, which passed by in each direction every day. Commerce expanded hugely. Grain was transported from far distant fields and mills to ever-hungry, ever-demanding Dublin, as was turf, cut laboriously by hand on the central boglands and sent up to fuel thousands of city fires. Dublin in return sent out those goods, foodstuffs, fabrics, hardware, farming tools, anxiously awaited by merchants

Mount Street Bridge at the start of the Grand Canal in Dublin.

and small shopkeepers in the countryside, as well as barrels of the black drink for which Ireland is famous. Young men and women who hitherto could see no opportunities beyond the fields around them, now grasped new chances to work with the canal boats, their associated industries, or their hotels.

Arthur Guinness wasn't precisely responsible for the Grand Canal, but he was certainly aware of its incipient arrival when he founded his family business at St James' Gate, and knew the use he could make of it. Landowners and merchants of towns some distance from the route of the canal used all their influence (and often their own money) to have links built to connect them to this new waterway that could make all the difference to their prosperity. And people from every county touched by the project began to travel themselves.

Before the coming of the canal in the late eighteenth century, travel was for the very few. The wealthy could journey to their country estates by horse and carriage, and there were stage coaches which connected major towns, but only for those who could afford the fare – and most couldn't. Roads were still in a very basic state, far removed from the smooth motorways to which we are accustomed today. Often they were no more than rough, muddy trackways with deep trenches where a coach could easily be marooned for hours if not days. The majority of the population stayed, lived, worked in the place where they had been born.

Now, however, it was possible to travel from one side of the country to the other, or from a small settlement along the way to either east or west. A journey which, even for the wealthy, was pleasurable because it removed the rattling, shaking, dust and mud which were inevitable concomitants of carriage journeys. For the less well off, it was novelty, comfort, and adventure combined. To see places you had never seen before, travel through strange countryside, meet up with relatives living far away, and under safe protected conditions – this was rich experience. And it was more affordable, at 1d or 1½d per mile rather than the 3d per mile charged by coach companies. Travelling outside your own region was at last achievable.

For businesses and farming families, it made a momentous difference, since goods and produce could now be shipped easily for far further distances than before. Instead of relying on selling your crops or your wool clip, your beer or your whiskey at local markets, you could send these to Dublin where they were always in demand. Or even onward from Ringsend to the UK and further afield. It was a whole new world.

The Grand Canal changed lives (as it will change yours, no matter how slightly, when you travel along its storied length). Not only could people travel longer distances, get to far-off places, but in their own villages they also came into contact with those building the canal (the 'navvies' or navigators, as they were called), got to know those who operated the barges, met travellers pausing for a night,. The superb canal hotels, where a fine lady and gentleman might disembark to stay, also offered rich opportunities for new forms of employment among local residents, as did the busy quaysides themselves. Catering for the demands and whims of wealthy travellers meant the hotels had to maintain a large staff of cooks, waiters, chambermaids, laundresses, and boot boys, as well as arranging reliable sources of quality foodstuffs. On the quays,

Lock C3 on the Grand Canal in Dublin.

clerks were needed to sell tickets, register packages and parcels for onward transport, and record goods brought to be kept in the spacious storehouses alongside. Ostlers, farriers, stable-boys were required to care for the horses that drew the boats, since these were changed at regular distances along the canal's route. And that meant supplies of hay, oats, straw too, to be purchased locally. Even small boys could earn pennies for carrying bags of hotel guests to and from their accommodation. Putting it in a nutshell, the coming of the Grand Canal made quite a difference to everyday life from the late eighteenth century onwards.

Walking this great long-distance pathway, you are following in the footsteps of those who went before, and indeed the hoofprints of plodding horses patiently towing the barges from one stop to the next. Check the arches under every bridge that you come to, and see if you can find the deeply-etched grooves where tow ropes grated against the stone and wore it away over decades. Watch for the ruined storehouses where grain and turf and other desirable goods were kept under lock and key until the next boat for Dublin came along. See the lock-keepers' cottages, sometimes renovated and brightly painted, sometimes in overgrown ruins. This was where a man and his family lived, employed to open and shut the lock gates, collect tolls where necessary, keep law and order if required (and it often was!). Look for the ivy-covered larger buildings near locks that once echoed to the clop of hooves and the soothing voices of ostlers leading in tired horses for a rest and bringing out fresh hoof-power to take the barge to its next stop.

Above all, walk through the serenely silent boglands that form the centre of Ireland. Here you will find that quietness and sense of unchanging time that is so rare in our lives these days. The wind blows over the grass and heather as it has always done, birds skim over the water, hares and rabbits dart out of sight. Wild flowers are as richly abundant as they were when the canal was first constructed, since the land has been undisturbed since.

Glance at the open skies above, see which way the clouds are blowing, assess what is indicated for the day ahead. It's a sad fact that we don't look at the skies for information any more, relying instead on bland forecasts relayed from a distant television studio under bright lights. It's more than time we got back to the old ways, the slow ways, and renewed our contact with the land we live in. Time to walk the Grand Canal Way.

You don't need instruction in the obvious: leave no litter, keep an eye out for local traffic, watch children and dogs near locks, which can have deep water. You would do that anyway, wouldn't you?

Lock C1 at Ringsend in Dublin.

A Brief History
OF THE
Canal

They were talking about it as early as 1715, but it was the middle of the century before work actually got going on the Grand Canal. It soon began to be seen that this was going to be an expensive undertaking. A small section near Sallins was completed before money ran out in 1768 and the entire project was abandoned for a while.

In 1772, The Grand Canal Company was formed to make a new start and tackle, among other problems, the considerable challenge of crossing the Bog of Allen. St James' Gate, the western boundary of the city, was chosen as the starting point. However, the actual work began at Clondalkin, some way outside, rather than in the city, as the ground was level there, whereas the descent towards St James' Gate would require the building of several locks.

1779 saw the St James' Gate to Sallins stretch finally opened. A twice-weekly passenger service was introduced on this section from 1780 and was well supported, people taking to this new and smooth mode of transport with evident pleasure.

By 1784, the canal had been extended to Robertstown, and a Grand Canal Hotel was opened here in 1806.

A branch to the south from Lowtown, just beyond Robertstown, to join with the Barrow river, was always part of the planning, since this would link the main line with the very important international port of Waterford. Work started on this in 1783; it had reached Monasterevin in 1785, and Athy in 1791, bringing barge traffic down to where it could merge with the river for its onward journey.

Originally the company had envisaged accessing the Liffey, and thus the open sea, close to St James' Gate, but this proved impracticable, and it was decided to cut a large semicircular link right round the city boundaries to Ringsend. Here a large canal basin and graving docks would be constructed to deal with barges coming down and ships coming in. Work started on this in 1790, and it was completed the following year as far as Portobello, which became the new terminus for passenger traffic. Ringsend docks opened in 1796, completing the Circle Line.

Crossing the Bog of Allen was every bit as difficult as envisaged, and certainly more costly than thought. In all it took over five years to get the canal dug, lined with clay to prevent leakage embanked, and filled. Even then, breaches occurred regularly. But by 1798, the line of canal had been completed to Tullamore.

In 1804, Shannon Harbour was finally reached and the canal fully opened for traffic. Overall it had taken 47 years to build and cost somewhere in the region of £877,000. So long had it taken, indeed, that a tiny cloud had already appeared on

The Leinster Aqueduct over the Liffey near Sallins.

the horizon: in February of that year, the first steam locomotive was run on a stretch of railway line in Wales.

In 1807, a new passenger terminus and hotel opened at Portobello in Dublin.

By 1810, canal trade was reaching 200,000 tons a year, and revenues from passenger boats had increased to £90,000.

1826 saw the first steamer travel all the way from Dublin through Shannon Harbour to Limerick.

In 1834, the first fly boats came into use: they used three or four horses instead of two, and travelled at a trot rather than a walk, thus reducing the time of journeys.

1851 brought the railway age, as the Dublin to Galway line was opened. It had an almost instant effect on passenger traffic on the canal, dropping numbers sharply.

In 1852, the passenger boats were withdrawn. Speed had taken over from slow and peaceful.

In 1911, the Grand Canal Company decided to try engine-propelled barges. First they tried a four-cylinder Scott Sterling engine, but this was not a success. Bolinder engines were tried next, and proved satisfactory, although there are many stories from bargemen who complained of the difficulty in starting and maintaining them. By the start of WWI, 28 former horse barges had been converted.

However, WWII brought the horses back again, since fuel was scarce. They worked throughout the Emergency, hauling much-needed loads of turf across the country.

In 1950, the canal and all its branches were taken over by Córas Iompair Éireann (CIÉ), the national transport company. In view of the vast expansion of road traffic, commercial business on the canal was gradually withdrawn at the end of that decade. 51M, the last working barge from Dublin, carried Guinness to Limerick on 27 May 1960, and the final boat from Limerick arrived in the capital on 14 June the same year. It was the end of an era.

Soon after, Dublin Corporation announced plans to drain the canal and replace it with a 6-lane dual-carriageway, utilising the canal bed for sewage pipes. The plans were strongly opposed, and eventually abandoned, thus saving this heritage for future generations.

Opposite: The Grand Canal meets the Shannon at last.

The old and the new: Bolands Mills at Ringsend.

eight*Chapter I*

ᴬLL ᴬROUND
———— THE ————
CITY

Y ou have to start the adventure down at Ringsend,
where the Grand Canal meets the Liffey. Even if you only
intend a short walk, a quick bicycle ride, this is where it all
begins. On foot or wheel, get down to Sir John Rogerson's
Quay and round to where you can see that big sign saying
Grand Canal, and the lock gates that gave access to ships
coming from the open ocean into a calm water basin. Inside
those lock gates are the old graving docks, where boats could
be repaired or repainted, and along the edges of the basin,
still surviving after more than 200 years, stand the great
warehouses which stored grain brought in on barges from
the fertile lands west of Dublin.

The water at the inner edge of Grand Canal Basin laps a
wonderful old cobbled quayside that takes you right back
to the late eighteenth century. Today it is a popular spot for

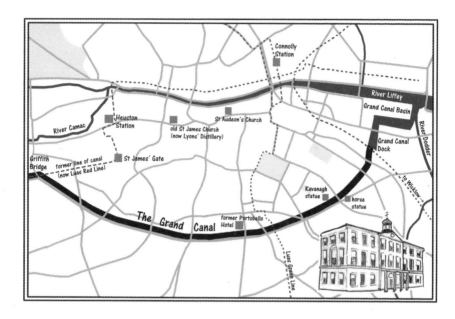

paddle boarders to enjoy their sport, but back in the early days of the canal, it would have been buzzing with activity – boats being unloaded, men running up and down gang-planks, horses and carts clattering in and out, emptying their loads, perhaps taking a different cargo on, and clip clopping out again. Barges laden with goods for transport across the country slipped their moorings, the horse boy chirruped to his charge, the towrope tightened, and they were off, moving slowly out of the basin and up to the canal proper.

It's a truly atmospheric place to visit, this cobbled quayside, a real glimpse back in time, but to continue the walk you need to follow Hanover Quay on the outer edge of the basin. Here high-profile companies occupy high-rise buildings, coffee shops abound, and there is always a busy, energetic ambience, which contrasts most effectively with the calm ripple of the water and the cobblestones on the other side. Grand Canal Quay runs past the Waterways Ireland building, which seems to float right on the water of Grand Canal Dock, surrounded by houseboats and converted barges. Stoop your head going under the extremely low bridge that carries the railway to Wicklow; cars can't pass under this, but you can on bicycle or on foot. It's a reminder that when the canal was built, railways hadn't yet been invented, let alone cars. By water was the way to go.

The canal soon makes a curve, and the large extra turning space in the water that a lumbering barge needed for this action can still be discerned, although it has now been filled in. The site bears the name Grand Canal Plaza though, so that its origins won't be forgotten.

There is a road to cross here (Grand Canal Street, unsurprisingly), and now you really are on to one of the most relaxing and charming stretches of this circular green route around the city. Opposite you, on the south side at Herbert Place, outside a commercial building, is a magnificent bronze statue of a barge horse and the boy who led him. Created by artist Maurice Harron, it is a tribute to those hard-working equines who toiled day after day, year after year, towing the barges up and down the canal from one side of the country to the other. It's a wonderful sight to glimpse across the glimmering water, adding to the serenity and the sense of history in this area.

Everywhere else in our capital city are traffic jams and exhaust fumes, busy crowds and packed buses, laden lorries and slow-moving articulated trucks, but here on the canal, life is still and calming and very beautiful. Mature trees line the banks,

Where it begins. The Grand Canal
Docks and locks at Ringsend.

their leaves reflected in the water. Ducks and moorhens scurry in and out of the reeds. And at Wilton Terrace, right on cue, there sits the poet Patrick Kavanagh on his bench, watching the canal and its life pass by, as he always loved to do.

> Oh, commemorate me where there is water
> Canal water, preferably …

It is the perfect place to stroll, push a buggy, talk with friends or enjoy the experience alone with a coffee from one of the many little cafes that have sprung up along the way.

Portobello is redolent with history, since here stands the finest surviving example of the Grand Canal hotels, built in 1807 to serve the increasing numbers of private passengers taking advantage of this new waterway to travel long distances.

Patrick Kavanagh dreams by the Grand Canal.

Hotels survive at other locations along the way, notably Robertstown and Shannon Harbour, but this one, currently an English language school, looks as good as it ever did, with that great Crostwaithe clock set high up on the frontage. And look at that car park next to the hotel. See how the back curves in a semicircle? That is the telltale sign that this was formerly the canal basin, where barges could moor and turn, allowing passengers to embark and disembark.

For Portobello, throughout the first half of the nineteenth century, was the main passenger terminus for the Grand Canal. At this point, travellers gathered to await the 10.20am to Tullamore or the 8.20am to Athy. They could watch the arrivals who had travelled overnight from those places and even further afield step wearily down the gangplank and make gratefully for the hotel. Special carriage services were offered to convey the wealthy to Portobello in time for the departures, and to take those just arrived to other points in the city. The charges were hefty enough for the service, at 2s2d per passenger, or 6s6d for taking up the entire coach. Presumably passengers were picked up at their city residences, which would at that time have been within quite a small radius.

At first, the only option was a slow barge, drawn by two horses, but later the company instituted faster 'fly boats', with several horses harnessed up. It was claimed at the time that the horses galloped the entire way along the towpath between stopping points, but this is very unlikely. The risk of crashes or upending the boat would have been far too likely. Probably the horses moved at a trot when they could, rather than a slow plod. Naturally enough, it cost more to travel on a 'fly boat'.

A bit like flying direct today rather than the cheaper option of several stops en route.

One lady who travelled by canal in the early nineteenth century published an account of her journey in her later years:

We arrived at the harbour of Portobello at a little after one o'clock, having been recommended to be early in the field, and secure comfortable seats near one of the doors of the cabin: but, early as we were, we were too late for that; as in one corner was already established a comfortable-looking Englishman, who begged he might be allowed to keep his seat by this door, as from it he could have the best view of the country as we passed along ... The cabin was a long, narrow apartment, along either side of which ran a bench, covered with red moreen, and hard enough to have been stuffed with paving stones, but I believe it was really with chopped hay, and capable of accommodating on each seat fifteen uncrinolined individuals, who might sit there comfortably enough on a cold winter's day, with a roaring turf fire in the small grate, as I have done more than once, while the boat was being slowly forced through a sheet of ice, several inches in thickness. But this was a hot holiday; and this same paved bench was, when night closed around, to serve us thirty poor travellers in the stead of beds, whereon to stretch our weary limbs. Between the seats ran a narrow table of about a foot-and-a-half in width, which was now covered with the small parcels of the passengers – books, boxes, baskets, dressing-cases, and, oh, horror! a cage, containing a fine singing canary.

After the boat had commenced its motion, and when all the passengers had taken their seats, we ascended on deck to enjoy

Latouche Bridge and the old Grand Canal Hotel at Portobello.

the fresh air, and admire the splendid action of the spanking steeds ambling along the bank (the towing-path is, I believe, the technical term) and which, fastened to our mode of conveyance by a tolerably thick rope, propelled it through the dark waters at the rapid rate of about three miles an hour. Several of the inmates of the down-stairs region had also turned out on deck, amongst them was a timid-hearted youth, who taking me under his guidance, introduced me to the second cabin, the company of which seemed preparing to be very merry and jovial, with the aid of a piper and a fiddler, who were already plying their art …

'A Canal Boat Sketch', *Duffy's Hibernian Sixpenny Magazine,*

January 1862

Portobello is a bustling part of Dublin city today, with crowds of people enjoying the scenery and the canal waters, but it would have been an even more thronged scene back when the canal was at its busiest. Think of all those excited or nervous travellers as you stroll the towpath of today's world up towards Dolphin's Barn and Griffith Bridge. Then stop, just before Suir Road Luas station, because this is quite an important point: the junction where the original line of the canal from St James' Gate joined the circular line on which you have been strolling. Look down there where the Luas line runs through a green linear park back towards the city. That rail track is built over the canal itself. In fact, if you take the Luas from Suir Road back into town towards Rialto or Fatima station, you will be travelling along the actual line of the first stretch of the original canal, which began at St James' Gate.

A peaceful canal scene in Dublin.

If history interests you, then do take that journey into town. Only a short distance on the Luas, but such a long way back in the story of this wonderful waterway, to the very spot where a company of Dublin investors bravely decided in the eighteenth century to dig a canal right across the central plains of Ireland, to meet the mighty Shannon on the other side.

Why did the Grand Canal start at St James' Gate in the first instance? Well, it was obvious really at the time. Today it may appear rather run-down, and is certainly in the midst of major development works, but in earlier times, this was the great western entrance to the medieval walled city, named for the nearby church of St James. Here goods brought in from the countryside were assessed for tolls before they could be sold on within the walls. West of this gate was the area known as The Liberties, where tolls could be avoided on goods because they were outside the city limits and thus its regulations. It is still known as The Liberties today.

St James' Gate was also the important and officially recognised departure point for pilgrims setting out to Santiago de Compostela in northern Spain. Having put their affairs in order (for there was no guarantee they would ever return from their holy journey), the determined faithful would go first to St Audeon's Church close by, to touch the Lucky Stone, believed to bring good fortune and a safe voyage. They would then pass through the gate, and down to the Liffey, where they boarded boats heading either for Spain (if they were lucky) or one of the French ports like Bordeaux, which kept Ireland supplied with wine and salt. The first route shortened the journey somewhat, as you were landed in the country of final destination; the

second necessitated a trek down to the Pyrenees and a dangerous climb over those peaks to reach the Spanish side. St James'
Gate itself was, sadly, demolished in the eighteenth century, but
the name remains on maps and in many other instances, as a
reminder of the city's early walls and guarded entrance gates.

St Audeon's, on the north side of High Street (itself one of
Dublin's earliest streets), is an absolute little gem, the oldest
medieval church in the city still in use. The Lucky Stone which
can be seen here is in fact a ninth-century grave-slab, showing
that a still earlier church stood on this land. Not just pilgrims,
but everyday citizens still pop in here to touch the stone and
bring themselves good luck for the day or the week. It's a very
old and firmly-held tradition in our capital city.

St Audeon's church, the oldest still in use in the city.

Nearby, the current church of St James (on the site of a much older building), having fallen into disuse, has, rather engagingly, been converted into a distillery, where tours are offered. There are some splendid stained glass windows here, depicting, inter alia, the pilgrimage to Santiago, thus keeping its origins alive. Nearby, the now legendary Guinness Storehouse also offers tours.

This is an area of the old city that brings you right back into the mists of time. In fact, the whole district in and around St James' Gate is absolutely steeped in history, and well worth exploring. Those who first put into motion the idea of a canal linking east and west, though many centuries later than the early pilgrims, were equally courageous in embarking on such a major enterprise. Where more fitting than at Dublin's western gate, where today the name of Guinness predominates?

The old entrance to the Guinness brewery at St James' Gate

As far as can be ascertained, Arthur Guinness did not have any specific involvement in that enterprise at its planning stage, but he was certainly aware of the project. He also knew what he was doing when he took over a failing brewery in this district, right beside the City Basin, which supplied drinking water to the city. Later, his brewery and his legendary product were to become a major part of the trade on the canal, and the very last commercial boat to ply thereon was a Guinness barge (51M), taking the final load of porter from Dublin to Limerick in 1960. During the busy years, it was always claimed that the porter shipped by canal had a special flavour because it had time to settle and mature on the leisurely voyage across country.

Alongside the trendy coffee shops and the historic buildings of this part of old Dublin, there are many signs of the earlier industrial days still surviving in great stone warehouses that stare out unsmilingly through gaunt barred windows. The original canal harbour, which began business in 1779, was where boats were moored and goods were loaded and unloaded. It is now filled in, but that defining curve, and indeed its name remain as echoes of the past. (Always keep an eye out for street names that might hold clues to former times.) An excellent idea of the harbour's original shaping and layout can be obtained from the top of the Guinness Storehouse. New developments may inevitably take over, but often the old can still be discerned if you look keenly with an eye that is willing to see.

From St James' Gate, the canal kept beside the old western route out of the city, and headed towards what is now Suir Road. This is where the older and the newer (so to speak) come together, as the original (now a Luas line) meets with the Circle Line coming all the way round the city from Ringsend.

So why, you might well ask, did the planners and developers, only a year or two into the massive and already expensive construction project, decide to build a ring canal right around the city to connect with Ringsend and the Liffey at its closest point to the sea?

Well, two factors influenced this major decision (which must have added a great deal to both planning angst and hard cash). First of all was trade. That was the original and principal purpose of the new canal, and it would have been intended right from the beginning to bring in overseas trading as well as cross-country transport. It became evident fairly quickly, though, that access to the Liffey at St James' Gate was not going to be as simple as they had hoped: local gentry were difficult about making their lands available for canal development, and the original idea of a direct descent by a series of locks was considered too challenging. And so, another location for accessing the Liffey would have to be found, and quickly too.

Secondly, passenger travel unexpectedly showed every sign of becoming popular. It hadn't been envisaged in the planning stages, but once it started happening, the company realised that here was a new source of profit and one which would deserve some attention. At first, both goods and passengers embarked on the canal at St James' Gate, and a hotel was built here for the convenience of travellers. The Liberator, Daniel O'Connell, remembered that very establishment in later years:

Barge horse and boy statue at Herbert Place.

… As we passed through St James'-street, he pointed out a dusky red brick house, with stone cornices and architraves, on the south side of the street. 'That,' said he, 'was the Grand Canal Hotel. One night in 1803 I searched every room in that house.' 'For what did you search?' 'For Croppies. I was then a member of the Lawyers' Corps, and constantly on duty.'

[Personal Recollections of the late Daniel O'Connell MP, by Wm J O'N Daunt, Chapman & Hall]

However, the well-to-do of Dublin did not consider this location at the city's western gate an appropriate place from which to embark, or indeed in which to stay the night, and put pressure on the company to provide a more pleasant, central option. This was duly provided at Portobello, where the Circle Line came through Rathmines. A new passenger terminus and a luxurious hotel were built here in 1807.

It was quite an achievement, to plan and build a linking canal right around the edge of the then existing city, but they did it in double quick time, opening the new Circle Line in 1796, and also creating a vast basin, graving docks, and lock gates at Ringsend, so that shipping from the open sea could come in and moor safely. It would not be possible today, but Dublin was smaller then.

GRAND CANAL// LINE OF COMMUNICATION
BETWEEN THE GRAND CANAL AND THE LIFFEY.
Notice is hereby given, that three or more Commissioners, duly appointed by Commission, under the common Seal of the Company of Undertakers of the Grand Canal, will attend at the Cross Keys in Christ Church-yard in the County of Dublin on Tuesday

the 27th Day of October instant, with a Jury of the said County of Dublin duly impannelled, and will proceed to a Valuation of the Estates and Interests of the several Proprietors and tenants of such Lands, Grounds, Houses and Premises in the County of Dublin as shall be made Use of for the making of the aforesaid Line of Communication. N.B. For the information of all Persons interested in said Lands and Grounds, the Whole of the Line is marked by a Circle cut in the ground in each Field, and the Canal and Banks will occupy five Perches outwards from said Mark. A Map of the Line may be viewed in the Hands of Mr Cudmore.

Saunders' Newsletter, 24 October 1789

All around the city. Of course, you can start at St James' Gate and then travel out to Griffith Bridge and Suir Road to wander the Circle Line round and down to Ringsend Docks. There are plenty of welcoming benches along the towpath, and dozens of coffee shops. What better way to spend a relaxing Sunday?

Meadowsweet frames an old barge

From the west to the city: The Grand Canal heading into Dublin.

GRIFFITH BRIDGE

—— TO ——

LUCAN

c. 11 km

With the roar of traffic all around, and buildings on every side, it's hard to imagine Griffith Bridge and its environs as peaceful and rural, with only the sound of sheep bleating to disturb the silence. But back in 1780, when the Grand Canal started its twice-weekly passenger service to Sallins, this was very definitely outside the city and in the country. One little road crossed the canal by this bridge, where the St James' St original line merged with the Circle line (at that time shown on local maps as the Ringsend Cut); otherwise the waterway proceeded gently westward, crossing the River Camuck

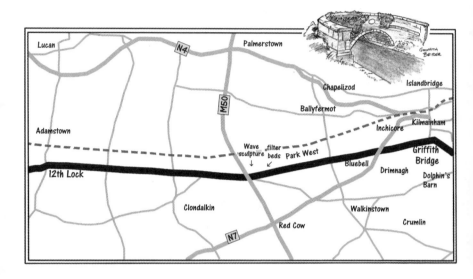

by Aqueduct Bridge and Black Horse Bridge (the original inn that gave the crossing its name is still there today), and more or less paralleling the old road towards Inchicore and all points west. There is a modern canal crossing today, more than capable of coping with the very heavy traffic it receives, but it's worth pausing to admire the cut limestone and granite piers of the single-arch span of Griffith Bridge, and the curve of stonework which brings one canal to meet the other. Often you will find a heron quietly fishing here, serenely unmindful of walkers and cyclists (not to mention the Luas line) passing by.

Kilmainham Gaol lies only about 750 metres to the north of Griffith Bridge. It's worth a visit to experience one of its guided tours, learn some of its harrowing history, and also see the remarkable architecture of this grim place. It's now a museum, with stories and exhibits about former prisoners, but back in 1796, when it first opened, it would have been eyed with curiosity and some fear by those passing on the canal. Among those held here were Robert Emmet, Anne Devlin, various Fenians, Charles Stewart Parnell, Countess Markievicz and the leaders of the 1916 Easter Rising, many of whom were executed by firing squad in the Stonebreaker's Yard there.

Not surprisingly, given its soaring spaces and relatively good state of repair, the gaol has been used for many films, among them *The Italian Job* in 1969 (remember Noel Coward masterminding the gold robbery from his cell?), *Michael Collins*, *The Wind That Shakes the Barley*, and even parts of *Paddington 2*. It lends itself surprisingly well to the movie world.

Goldenbridge, even closer to the canal than Kilmainham, has an unusual burial ground, The Old Goldenbridge Cemetery.

Eighteenth-century Griffith Bridge by Suir Road.

Daniel O'Connell founded it and called it non-denominational, so Catholics could bury their dead there. Otherwise, in those penal times, they had to be interred in Protestant cemeteries, and mourners were prevented from praying at the graves.

It is hardly a kilometre of pleasant strolling, past Locks 1 and 2, to reach the fringes of Inchicore. Spreading over a huge area, with wide-reaching complexes of tracks and buffers, shunting zones and signal posts, Inchicore is inescapably associated with Irish Rail, the transport method that took over almost entirely from canal travel. In older times, though, travellers would have seen a much more pastoral landscape. Its name derives from the Irish *Inis Caoire*, or Land of the Sheep, since large flocks were put to graze in the fields here, before being driven into the city markets.

Not much space for even a lamb these days, but despite the intensive development everywhere, the canal winds peacefully past industry and commerce, much as it did back in the late eighteenth century, when the only sounds to be heard were the shouts of the boys leading the towing horses or a call from a friend on the bank waving to passengers on board.

From here, the Grand Canal heads west into the far distance. For many early travellers, this was completely new territory, giving views over fields and hedgerows, little cottages and hamlets they had never seen before. It was travelling, exploring, experiencing on a grand scale and must have created many memories to be recalled later on in life, or to tell to children when they arrived at their destination.

An account by an unidentified gentleman, which appeared in the *Dublin Evening Packet* over several issues in the summer

A grey heron hunts for dinner in the canal, just as his forefathers did.

of 1831, describes the experience of leaving the city, under the heading of 'The Delights of West Dublin':

The scenery along this part of the canal is particularly interesting. A row of very fine beech trees, now attained to their full growth, is planted on each bank, and the overhanging branches present a delightful retreat from the summer's sun to the pedestrian rambler, while the winter's blast loses much of its force as it spends its fury against these formidable barriers.

The country, on the left hand, is richly cultivated; the fields, beautifully green, are interspersed with groves waving with thick luxuriant foliage. Neat villas, the summer residences of our Dublin citizens, are numerously spread over the landscape; two or three spires of churches, the tops of which are seen rising above the other buildings, present a variation of character to the surrounding prospect; while that splendid and gorgeous line of mountain which separates the counties of Dublin and Wicklow, glowing now in all the loveliness and true nobility of mountain scenery – a ray of light breaking forth from beneath a cloud, and exhibiting to view a deep and rugged or some cottage before observed, now lying in thick shadow awful amidst its grandeur – gives a finish to the back-ground of the picture, but seldom seen throughout nature's kingdom.

Walking the canal bank today gives the opportunity to create memories of our own, be it of the sparkling water, the time-worn stonework, the lush grass and plants along the way, or simply the feeling of being away from the hustle and bustle of the modern world, in an earlier, more peaceful time.

That is one of the real benefits of taking the Grand Canal Way – you really do get away from it all.

Now the Naas Road passes overhead, but you hardly notice it, enjoying instead the marker points of Locks 3, 4 and 5 with their carefully maintained paintwork of black and white and the water gushing through each set of gates into the lock basin, where boats would wait to be lifted up or down to the next level. That's the reason for locks – canals have to run on the level, to keep the water at the same depth, but the countryside is undulating, and so something has to be done to enable water traffic to pass from one level to another. Locks are nothing new – they had them in ancient China – but it's very nice to see them still in place and even operating in some cases, here today. At some point along the Grand Canal, you will see boats being 'locked through' – it's well worth pausing to watch how it is done.

Echoes of the past: A long-abandoned mooring ring.

Past Lock 6 to New Bridge, with Bluebell and elegant thirteenth-century Drimnagh Castle away to the south (the only remaining castle in Ireland with a flooded moat around it, fed by that same River Camuck that the canal crossed earlier). Next, Lock 7, where Killeen Road bridges the canal, and now, between this and Lock 8, you are passing the gigantic business centre known as Park West on your north side.

Although you wouldn't think it as you stroll or cycle along your private green way, this development comprises huge numbers of offices and retailers, as well as a hotel, a private hospital, and apartment complexes. A central feature, right on the canal side, is Europe's tallest wind and water mobile sculpture, Wave. Created by Angela Conner, it's 39.3 metres (129 feet) tall and indeed conveys the movement of both elements in its design.

Near to Lock 8 are the filter beds, still used as a water supply by Guinness at its James' St brewery. (There are filter beds used by Dublin city to supply water too, back near to Lock 5). The old legend used to be that Guinness took Liffey water to create its famous porter, but that was never true. The brewery was established on a local stream at St James' Gate, but later the company created filter beds out here and drew additional supplies via pipes from those. In case you are concerned about tonight's anticipated pint, be assured that the canal water, though certainly filtered, is only used for cleaning the vats these days!

But how can a city and a brewery use canal water? Wouldn't that drain the canal and stop all traffic? Well, it all has to do with what are known as 'feeders' – the local rivers that were directed to the canal as it was dug, and supplied its water. Of itself, a canal doesn't have any natural source. It relies on the feeders to keep its levels up, and locating and utilising these rivers was an essential part of the whole planning and digging process back in the second half of the eighteenth century.

Now you might hear a roar of heavy traffic ahead, and glance up to spare a smug thought for hard-pressed commuters, lorry drivers, tankers, as the M50 thunders overhead

The filter beds at Park West used by Guinness.

The Wave kinetic sculpture at Park West.

in its never-ending procession. It hardly registers though, as you try to identify that birdsong or pause to look at a wild rose trailing over the hedgerow. We're in a different world here, far from the harsh realities of tarmac and traffic jams.

Ahead and to your left (to the south), a tall structure can be seen in the distance. That is the famous round tower of Clondalkin, thought to be the oldest in the country. Founded by St Mochua, it is one of only four remaining round towers in Co. Dublin. Thought to have been built around 790 AD, the tower stands at 27.5 metres high. It still has its original cap, and is thought to be the most slender of all such structures in Ireland. Its height and evident defensive capability is a reminder that Clondalkin suffered its share of vicissitudes during its long history.

The tower was attacked by Vikings in 833, when the monastery here was plundered and burned. Two further attacks in later years were by local chieftains, while it was ransacked by Brian Boru's troops in 1014, before the Battle of Clontarf. It saw battle again during the Norman invasion, when Strongbow fought with Rory O'Connor, the last High King of Ireland.

Locks 9 and 10 lie close together here, where a short walk (less than 1km) will take you into the centre of the town. Of course it is now a vastly expanded suburb of Dublin, but at its heart it still preserves the original village, with narrow streets and laneways holding a pleasurable array of little shops and cafes, just right for a break from walking. It has in fact been settled since Neolithic times and so has seen every stage of this country's development.

An interesting fact: Clondalkin is where the first stages of digging the entire Grand Canal, east to west, was started. It might seem like a strange place to begin, neither at one end nor the other, but topography dictated the choice. From here down to Griffith Bridge and beyond, there is a drop of about 100 feet. Canal barges, by their very nature, cannot chug uphill and freewheel down, so quite a series of locks were going to be required, ten in all on that stretch into the city. Best to start on a level bit.

One can imagine the gathering together of all the engineers, and then the assembling of vast numbers of labourers with their picks, shovels and barrows, to start the actual hard work of clearing the ground and digging the trench along the line indicated by the engineers. And it would not have been plain digging on a clear patch of ground either. Ireland's landscape, left to itself, is a tangle of trees, shrubs, bushes and brambles, with rocks everywhere, and sudden dips and hillocks. Those first workmen would have had to clear all of that first, hacking down gorse bushes and swearing at long prickly brambles, before piling the greenery into heaps for later burning. Only then could they start on the digging below ground.

What did they get paid? It is a sad fact that very little information has survived on those who did the actual manual work. We can find plenty on the company directors, the lords and landowners involved, even the top engineers, but for the vast crews of labourers who toiled with shovel and barrow, we don't even have individual names. Just a stray mention here and there gives us a few clues. In April 1790, when work was at its height on this major long-distance project, the 'navvies' struck

Eighth-century Clondalkin round tower, thought to be the oldest in the country.

for eleven pence a day, which means they were at that time receiving somewhat less – say 8d or 9d. In June of that same year, severe working conditions and (possibly) the shortage of manpower gave them the impetus to strike again, this time for thirteen pence a day. Which they got. It is well nigh impossible to calculate such minor amounts by today's rates, but at the same time the chief engineers were being paid exceptionally large sums.

For example, as far back as 1772, John Trail was awarded the contract to complete the canal from the city basin to Sallins. For this he would receive five percent of all the money expended on the work – £300 per annum, and the balance when the contract was completed. In 1780, Richard Evans, an assistant engineer, received an extra gratuity of £70

A mute swan stretching his wings at Lucan Bridge.

Lock 12 on the Grand Canal at Lucan, with Shackleton's Mill.

Heading west from Lock 12.

over and above his salary, 'as a Proof of our Opinion of his Integrity and Attention to the Works of the Company'.

On past Lock 11, and now the end of this section is in sight, with Lucan Bridge and Lock 12, where the old Shackleton's Mill still stands. The mill was purchased by the family (ancestors of the Antarctic explorer Sir Ernest Shackleton) in 1848, some years before they acquired Anna Liffey Mill at Lucan. Shackletons is still a major company today, with its headquarters at Ashbourne in Co. Meath, but the old mill at Lock 12 stands as a reminder that everyone has to start somewhere.

There is a rather nice little lock keeper's house here too, designed by Thomas Omer, a Dutchman who was very much involved in both the planning and the construction of the Grand Canal and felt that the buildings should be as carefully designed as the waterway. Occasionally this got him into trouble with the company, as he tended to think rather casually of the increased costs in construction.

Although it is called Lucan Bridge, the town itself is almost 3km away to the north. Lucan was a famous spa town in its day, attracting thousands of visitors both from Dublin and further afield to take its waters and enjoy the lively social scene there, reminiscent of Bath or Baden Baden.

Closer to the canal is Adamstown, a new town set up in recent decades and still developing. Part of that development was the installation of a railway station – a rarity indeed when so many have closed – so you have the option of either starting your journey here or using the train to return to base. Up to you! So much more lies ahead.

Teazels grow wild at Gollierstown Bridge.

Chapter III

ℒUCAN

—— TO ——

SALLINS

c.17km

From Lucan Bridge, it's about 4.5km to Hazelhatch, and the nice thing about this stretch is that you are in open country. There is nary a road to be seen either side, just the Dublin–Cork railway line in the distance to the north (so you can wave to the passengers as they are whisked past). Apart from that, it's just you, the Grand Canal and the lovely countryside.

First the canal runs west to Gollierstown Bridge, a particularly lovely old structure with deep rope grooves cut into the arches underneath by the ropes of so many barges passing up and down over the centuries. The stone used to build it came

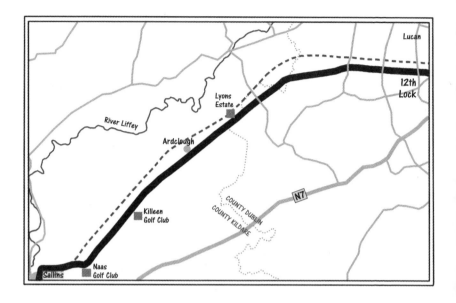

from quarries close by. Indeed, Thomas Omer, mentioned at the end of the previous chapter, insisted that the canal should be routed right by those quarries, as he saw the benefit of having good cut stone readily available to build the canal walls and bridges.

Today the bridge stands remote, simply connecting two grazing fields rather than carrying a road, but in its time, it saw plenty of traffic to and from the now deserted village of Gollierstown, now no more than a handful of ivy-covered ruined cottages. At the time of Griffith's Valuation though (about 1847), there were some fifteen residents, practically all of whom worked for or paid rent to the Grand Canal company.

Gollierstown may well have had its origins in one of the many temporary settlements which sprang up all along the banks of the canal as it was being dug in the late eighteenth and early nineteenth centuries. Hundreds of labourers were required for this exhausting work, and that in turn would have created the demand for food, accommodation and all the other needs of a community. From the point of view of the gentry, putting the labouring crews out here, some distance from the fashionable spa town of Lucan, was probably preferable to having them close at hand, since there were tales told of fights, drunkenness, and other disturbances wherever such labouring gangs were living. Hardly surprising really: given the backbreaking work they did all day, the few hours of relaxation in the evening would hardly be spent quietly.

It's a nice experience to come across Gollierstown Bridge today as you walk along, since now it stands quietly alone, seeming to be there just for you to enjoy, not for any practical

Once a busy crossing, now deserted: Gollierstown Bridge.

modern-day usage. Back a couple of centuries, though, it must have been a hive of activity, and if you listen with your inner ear, you might catch echoes of that past. The nearest centre of population is the very new community of Adamstown to the north, already mentioned in the previous chapter, where the railway station offers the choice of starting or finishing your day's journey here. Do check the times of stopping trains, though!

About halfway to Hazelhatch, the canal bends somewhat to the southwest. It continues in this direction until you reach Hazelhatch Bridge itself, crossed by the R405 and within walking distance of another railway station (again a very useful facility to note).

Hazelhatch might seem at first glance like a fairly small place, but it does have some interesting features. First, there are a number of brightly painted and well-maintained houseboats moored here, which are actually used as domestic dwellings by Dublin suburbanites. Some people just prefer a home on the water rather than on land.

It's a good place to live, one resident says, since you can see all kinds of wildlife. He often glimpses otters fishing and coming up on the grassy banks to enjoy their catch, while ducks paddle around the residential boats, keeping a sharp eye out for crumbs and scraps. There is a traditional pub here too, which does a good trade, especially with walkers and cyclists at weekends, hungry and thirsty after their journey along the canal.

Behind the pub there are some ivy-covered ruins that might not warrant a second glance, but which hold a history of their

You can still grow vegetables on a barge! Hazelhatch.

own, intrinsically linked to the story of the Grand Canal. These were stables, where the barge horses were changed, rested, fed, looked after, had shoes replaced, harness mended, injuries tended to. Since the early barges were all towed by horses, usually two to a barge (engines didn't come in until the mid-nineteenth century and during both world wars, when fuel was scarce, horses came back into their own again), there had to be stabling points at every official stop along the canal, with different suppliers of equine power at each stop. Newspaper advertisements by the Grand Canal Company in the late eighteenth and early nineteenth centuries frequently requested tenders for supplying horses for the various stages.

A popular mooring place by the pub at Hazelhatch.

(The private barges that used the canal to take grain or turf to Dublin, and goods from the capital out to the country towns, used their own horses.)

For example, *Saunders Newsletter* of 4 July 1822 ran the following advertisement:.

The Court of Directors of the Grand Canal are ready to receive Proposals for supplying able HORSES, to Draw the Company's Passage Boats to and from the following Stages, for three years, from the first day of August 1822: Tullamore to Shannon Harbour / Shannon Harbour to Tullamore. The Proposals to be sent to the Grand Canal House, William-street, before the twentieth July, 1822.

And again, in the *Dublin Evening Post* of 18 October 1825, the company requested proposals for the provision of horses *'to draw the Company's Passage Boats on the several Stages between Sallins and Robertstown, Robertstown and Ticknevin, and Ticknevin and Ballybritan, or any of said Stages, for three Years, commencing 1st November next'*.

Is it possible to work out from these advertisements just how far a hardworking horse was expected to pull a barge along the towpath before getting a well-earned rest?

Well, Sallins to Robertstown is some 12km, but Robertstown to Ticknevin is a much more demanding 27km. Ticknevin to Ballybrittan is slightly less, at 22km. Tullamore to Shannon Harbour is a hefty 34km. So it isn't all that easy to work out the distance these poor animals were expected to haul the barges laden with passengers and freight. Certainly the deep grooves worn into the sides of so many bridges are witness to the tightly strained ropes that they uncomplainingly pulled to move the heavy craft. It is much more likely that there were intervening halts along the way, not mentioned in the official lists, where goods and passengers could be dropped off and the horses changed.

Whatever the distance, the stables at each stop had to have reliable supplies of hay, oats and straw, to feed and comfort their four-legged guests. In addition, there would have been many workers required – ostlers, grooms, farriers, vets or at least men with equine medical experience, and of course stable boys. So there were plenty of opportunities for the local people along the way to profit from the stables, whether by supplying hay and straw or by getting jobs working with these valuable animals, without whom the boats would simply lose their motive power.

About 1.5km west of Hazelhatch, you come to Aylmer Bridge, named for the Aylmer family of Donadea demesne (but also known as Kearneystown Bridge, after the nearby town). This bridge, however named, marks the start of the boundary wall of the once great old Lyons estate, now owned and managed by UCD. It was an Irish wool merchant and banker, one Nicholas Lawless (afterwards Lord Cloncurry), who built Lyons House here in the 1780s, having purchased the estate from the Aylmers. His son Valentine was chairman of the Grand Canal Company and built the Lyons Mill (later owned by the Shackletons) and the lockyard complex.

In the nineteenth century, this was one overnight option as a stopping place for barge travellers. Today, the luxury Cliff

Above: Anglers, walkers, cyclists, all enjoy the Grand Canal.

Below: Deep grooves left by towing ropes at Aylmer Bridge.

at Lyons hotel backs right on to the canal towpath, offering welcome refreshments to tired hikers and cyclists in an excellent café.

The high protecting wall of the estate follows the towpath to Lock 13 (a double), originally designed by the lavish Thomas Omer to be 20 feet wide. John Trail, when he took over as engineer, thought that too wide and redesigned it to 14 feet. You can still see part of the old lock in the upper chamber..

To stand by the thirteenth lock and look west, down the considerable slope ahead, is to realise what locks are all about. Canals have to run on the level, whereas the countryside is anything but even. Hills, dales, sudden dips and rises may be taken for granted when you are walking (except perhaps for a puff or a gasp on steeper inclines), but they won't do for a canal. And so double locks like the thirteenth cope with the different heights, lifting and dropping the waterway up or down in the most even manner possible.

Close by is Cnoc Liamhna (Lyons Hill), said to be the inauguration site for the Uí Dúnchada, kings of Leinster a thousand years ago. Next, Oughterard (not to be confused with the town of the same name in Connemara!), an old religious hilltop site, can be seen rising some way back from the south bank of the canal. This is where Arthur Guinness (yes, the man who started it all!) is buried. Ardclough village houses a museum and an exhibition on the great figure, called, appropriately, From Malt to Vault. It's in what used to be the village school.

A splendid old tree on the Lyons estate by the Grand Canal.

The double Lock 13.

Ardclough is known for breeding superb racehorses today, but in the nineteenth century it was a busy spot for industry and commerce, with the Grand Canal carrying huge amounts of freight – around 90 barges a day passed through. Walking along the towpath in this quiet landscape, it sometimes seems possible to hear on the wind the bustle of boats and voices, the clip clop of hooves, the sounds of yesteryear.

Henry Bridge is in the centre of Ardclough village. Boatmen traditionally referred to this as the Eleven Mile Bridge, as it was 11 Irish miles from James' Street Harbour. About 2.5km on comes Ponsonby Bridge, with Devonshire Bridge about the same distance beyond that, followed shortly by the fourteenth lock. The lock keeper's cottage here has been well restored and is now privately owned; not so at the fifteenth lock, where only the ruins of a once busy and important premises are visible.

The all-important River Morrell feeder enters the canal between Devonshire Bridge and Lock 14. This river had (and still has) the all-important task of keeping the canal water levels up. In the early days, and indeed for over 90 years (until 1869), the Morrell, believe it or not, was also the principal source of drinking water for the people of Dublin. The water was piped all that way along the line of the canal.

Tipperstown at Henry Bridge was where the Tipper family had not just one, but two castles, which were burnt during the 1641 Rebellion. You can still see the ruin of the Reeves Tower House, but it is in private hands and so not approachable without permission. Henry Bridge itself dates from 1796 and is notable for possessing a 'squinch'. A what? In architecture, a squinch is 'a triangular corner that supports the base of a dome. Its visual purpose is to translate a rectangle into an octagon.' Maybe standing below the span and looking hard will make that clearer.

Gardens of The Cliff at Lyons hotel by the canal.

The fifteenth lock comes into view as the canal crosses Sherlockstown Common and passes Killeen Golf Club. Now Sallins is almost in sight. The canal curves right and heads under the Dublin–Cork railway line (a train is almost sure to pass if you take your time, and it's always fun to see). It then makes almost an S-bend to Sallins Bridge, conveniently close to the railway station, which offers another option for breaking a trip or starting a new stretch of the Grand Canal.

Sallins is a nice place to wander around and take in the atmosphere of other days. The first passenger boats arrived here, towed by those patient horses, in 1779, and from then on, the small harbour was always busy with boats loading and unloading at the huge Odlums Mill and other warehouses and stores. One of those great canal hotels was built here too, for the comfort of wealthy travellers, but once the waterway extended further out across the midlands, and passengers could travel further, business fell off. The once-proud accommodation was degraded to becoming a fish processing factory and then a meat plant, before eventual demolition in the late twentieth century.

You can still see old warehouses here though, and imagine how active life must have been back then, and how people were employed in keeping all the different facets of business going, from tending barge horses to checking grain loads and taking payments or issuing tickets for freight or human travel.

Opposite: A pied wagtail with canal boats at Sallins.

'We'll be there before tea.'

Chapter IV

SALLINS

—— TO ——

ROBERTSTOWN

*c.*12km

Just beyond Sallins, where the main road between Naas and Clane crosses the canal, is an extremely picturesque pub, called Lock 13. It is very popular with those coming out from the city at the weekend, and (understandably, given its threatening number) legend has it that it is haunted. However, it isn't actually at Lock 13. That was the double, well back at the Lyons estate. And there isn't a lock here at all, on this straight and calm stretch of water, just plenty of brightly painted canal boats. Still, it's an attractive name, and certainly gains it attention.

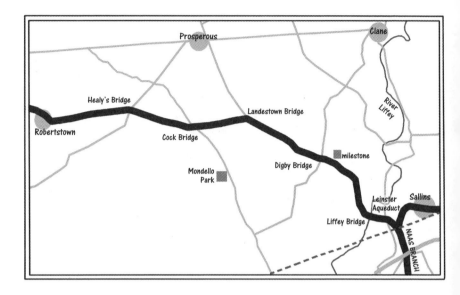

Beyond this, the canal turns sharp south, and then west again at the junction with the Naas and Corbally branch at leafy little Soldier's Island. The Naas branch deserves a little attention to itself. It's a nice little side route (no more than 3.5km down to Naas Harbour) and worth doing some time when you haven't the time (or the energy) for a longer stint on the main line.

THE NAAS BRANCH

Any late eighteenth- or early nineteenth-century merchant along the route who possessed both money and foresight was keen to get a branch of the Grand Canal cut through to his town. The possibilities for extending business, exporting locally produced goods and importing others, growing into a major player in the expanding world of commerce, were enormous.

The old harbour in Naas.

Dug and built by an independent company in 1786 to facilitate traffic to and from the already busy town of Naas, this short link carried freight and passengers up to Sallins and thence, by connecting into the main canal line, onward either east or west, to Dublin or the Shannon. Ambitiously, it was extended further down from Naas another 8km or so, to Corbally, but this stretch was never very successful.

Huge milling industry had grown up around these central plains where grain was grown plentifully. The coming of the Grand Canal made this possible since the grain could be transported effectively and cheaply to the mills, and the resultant flour or meal shipped onwards to Dublin or across the midlands to the west coast.

The Leinster Mills were set up in 1790 by Oldstown landlord James Montgomery. Just a year after the opening of the Naas branch of the Grand Canal, Montgomery cunningly negotiated a deal for the perpetual water rights to turn his millwheel. There is evidence of a mill in the area prior to this, while water wheels also turned at Corban's mill in Millbrook and Fryar's mill in Oldtown.

Eventually the short Naas branch itself fell into disuse, but in more recent years it has seen a revival through the Inland Waterways Association of Ireland. Now boats can enjoy its attractions once more, especially during the Canal Festival held each October. The little harbour in the centre of the town is a charming contrast to the roar of traffic and the relentless energy of modern-day commerce outside its quiet oasis.

BACK TO THE GRAND CANAL

Sticking with the main route, next comes a real architectural marvel, the dramatic five-arched Leinster Aqueduct. This is where the canal is carried right over the river Liffey below. It is a delight to walk, looking down from aloft on the bubbling river that seems so much more rural and lively here than when it flows in wide grey majesty through central Dublin. In fact, when building works were ongoing in the 1780s, the Liffey was utilised by the engineer in charge to bring up the building material for the aqueduct.

No doubt about it, the Leinster Aqueduct was quite an engineering feat for its time, long before today's technology, and it still inspires wonder in those who see and walk it.

The Leinster Aqueduct, a splendid engineering feat.

Far from the motorway. Sailing along the the Grand Canal.

Those hikers or cyclists fortunate with their timing might find a barge coming through, bringing a group on a sight-seeing tour from Sallins. Walking alongside, you can eavesdrop on the stories being told and the facts being related.

Now the towpath skirts a ridge of high ground, from which you can enjoy wide views over the valley. First swinging to the right, and then to the left (all of these bends were made necessary by the terrain through which it was dug), it passes under Digby Bridge to the sixteenth lock. This is another of those peaceful little oases where one can rest awhile and watch the water bubbling through the gates. (Incidentally, there is another Digby Bridge east of Tullamore, at the twenty-fifth lock, so don't confuse them if you are asking somebody to pick you up!)

Just before Digby Bridge, on the north bank of the canal, keep your eyes peeled and you will spot a lovely original milestone, marked to show that it is 16 English miles from

St James' Gate. North bank milestones were carved in English miles, those on the south bank in Irish miles. That way, nobody could argue about the tolls to be paid for the distance they had travelled (well, they probably did, but the milestones were there to measure the distance accurately and settle all disputes). And, just to answer that unspoken question, English miles were (still are) 5,280ft, but an Irish mile was at that time 6,720ft, quite a bit longer than that of our neighbours. It's up to you whether you decide to compute the distances you've walked or cycled in Irish or English lengths! There is usually a little coffee hut at Digby Bridge where refreshments can be obtained.

Beyond this, it's just about 1km to Landenstown Bridge, where the canal curves left to the seventeenth lock. On the opposite side of the canal is the gate into Landenstown estate, where Landenstown House was built for the Digbys around 1740.

Digby Bridge, by the 16th lock.

The family, apart from being land owners in Kildare, at one stage also owned the Aran Islands but didn't live there, preferring to rent out the lands through an agent. The Landenstown estate is now a major stud farm.

There's barely 1km to stroll before reaching the eighteenth lock, which has a significance all its own. It is the last step to the summit level or highest point of the main line of the Grand Canal. From this stretch, 279 feet above the sea at Dublin Bay, the headwaters of the canal divide to east and west. Stand and look back before tackling the next 1.5km to Cock Bridge (also known as Burgh Bridge).

Mondello Park lies just south of here, but if you hear the roar of racing engines, just ignore them and watch instead for the bright flash of a kingfisher speeding past. And don't forget to look for the deeply etched rope grooves that have been carved into the stonework of the arches over the years

Weatherworn milestone by Digby Bridge

You have to be quick to spot a kingfisher when it perches briefly

by countless thousands of horses dragging tightly-stretched ropes attached to heavy barges, past the bridge, a telling reminder of the canal's working past.

Some 2km further on is Healy's Bridge (also known as Bonynge Bridge). This was where John Wesley, the great Methodist preacher, and the first canal traveller to leave an account of his journey, left the canal boat to go up to Prosperous to preach. He thought highly of the canal:

Wednesday 22nd of June, 1785, I went with twelve of fourteen of our friends on the canal to Prosperous. It is a most elegant way of travelling little inferior to that of Tracksuyts in Holland. We had fifty of sixty persons in the boat, many of whom desired me to give them a sermon. I did so, and they were all attention.

From Healy's Bridge the canal and its towpath are raised above the level of the surrounding bogland, carried on a high earthwork. It is said, in fact, that the entire canal project nearly came to grief in this particularly difficult stretch of bog over the couple of km between Healy's Bridge and Robertstown. This wetland area is known charmingly as The Bog of Moods, but not, alas, from a habit of changing its attitude every five minutes. Rather it reflects its proximity to Mood's Well close by. And now the canal veers sharp right to enter Roberts-town at last.

Across on the left bank here stands one of the most strik-ing sights on the Grand Canal, the splendid hotel dating from 1801 and still dramatically dwarfing everything else in the village, despite being empty for many years and much in need of repair. Above the doorway with its graceful fan-light, and the wide flight of stone steps that so many weary passengers must have ascended and descended, sits the large Crosthwaite clock that was fitted to every company hotel along the waterway. The clocks were designed and made by master clockmaker James Crosthwaite. Originally from Athy, Crosthwaite later moved to Dublin and set up his business at Grafton Street.

The Crosthwaite clocks were a very important feature of the hotel and indeed the whole canal system relied on them. Without accurate timekeeping, or some way in which trav-ellers or merchants could check the time, it would not have been possible to keep to any kind of schedule as confidently advertised in the newspapers, as for example:

Sky and trees reflected in the canal water by Bonynge Bridge.

GRAND CANAL. Notice is hereby given that two Passage Boats will regularly, on and after the 25th Day of March instant, ply upon the Canal on every Day in the Week, Sundays not excepted; the one to leave Dublin on every Week Day, from the 25th instant to the 29th Day of September next, at seven o'Clock PRECISELY, and on Sunday at eight o'Clock PRECISELY; and the other to leave Sallins on every Day in the Week at eight o'Clock PRECISELY. The Boat setting from Dublin to reach Sallins at Half after twelve o'Clock on every Week Day, and at Half after one on every Sunday PRECISELY; and the Boat setting off from Sallins to reach Dublin at Half after one o'Clock PRECISELY on every Day in the Week.

Saunders' Newsletter, 24 March 1784

There were six of these hotels, constructed originally in the late eighteenth and early nineteenth centuries: James' Street and Portobello in Dublin, then Sallins, Robertstown, Tullamore and Shannon Harbour. We have an idea of how much some of them cost to build, from records of the time: Tullamore £4,391; Shannon Harbour £5,058; Portobello an exceptionally high £10,483 (but this included furnishing the building as well, presumably in sumptuous manner).

That great transport innovator, Bianconi (it is tempting to see him as the Ryanair of his day), was always quick to pick up on opportunities. He swiftly set up connecting routes to link with the passenger barges, so that those alighting at points like Robertstown could be taken on to other locations without delay, while travellers from distant towns could be brought to the quayside in time for the next boat to Dublin or Shannon Harbour.

What was it like, staying in those fine canal hotels? Well, of course they were advertised as providing every comfort, and for their time they probably did offer a pleasant alternative to catching a nap on a hard wooden seat on board the barge. Charges could range from a hefty 4s 4d for a 'best bedchamber' through a somewhat more affordable 2s2d for a shared room, down to 10d for servants' quarters. Clearly not for the impoverished. But, predictably, some clients weren't too pleased with the accommodation, notably a gentleman who published a detailed account of his vicissitudes in the *Dublin University Magazine* in 1842.

… Unlike any other hotel I had ever seen, there was neither stir nor bustle, no burly landlord, no buxom landlady, no dapper waiter with napkin on his arm, no pert-looking chambermaid with a bed-room candlestick. A large hall, dirty and unfurnished, led into a kind of bar, upon whose unpainted shelves a few straggling bottles were ranged together, with some pewter measures and tobacco pipes; while the walls were covered with placards, setting forth the regulations for the 'Grand Canal Hotel' with a list, copious and abundant, of all the good things to be found therein, with the prices annexed; and a pressing entreaty to the traveller, should he not feel satisfied with his reception, to mention it in a 'book kept for that purpose by the landlord.'

I cast my eyes along the bill of fare, so ostentatiously put forth – I read of rump-steaks and roast-fowls, of red rounds and sirloins, and I turned from the spot resolved to explore further. The room opposite was large and spacious, and probably destined for the coffee-room, but it also was empty; it had neither chair nor table …

Heading for the kitchen, he had no better luck:

> ... the goodly grate, before which should have stood some of that luscious fare of which I had been reading, was cold and deserted; in one corner, it was true, three sods of earth, scarce lighted, supported an antiquated kettle, whose twisted spout was turned up, with a misanthropic curl at the misery of its existence. I ascended the stairs, my footsteps echoed along the silent corridor, but still no trace of human habitant could I see, and I began to believe that even the landlord had departed with the larder.

The writer does not specify the location, but as, later on, he decides to walk to Loughrea rather than embrace the somewhat limited comforts of the hotel, it was probably Shannon Harbour.

There are also frequent complaints in the newspapers of the time about hotels being fast shut when the boat arrived late in the evening, and disembarking passengers, expecting warmth and comfort, instead being forced to seek shelter in sheds or barns until morning. The Grand Canal Company had had the hotels built, and operated them personally for a brief time, but then found it easier to lease them out to landlords, trusting the latter to ensure that a high standard was maintained at all times.

Although the great days of the passenger and freight boats have long passed, there is a real charm to Robertstown today for the walker or cyclist coming upon its serene setting. The shops are well stocked, there are always little brightly painted vessels moored at the quaysides, and there is a general air of holiday about the cheerful village. It's a nice place to linger and think of its importance in earlier times.

Beyond Robertstown, there is a major canal junction, where the Barrow Line leaves the main route and takes a southerly journey towards Athy. That branch is the subject of the next chapter, after which we rejoin the Grand Canal to continue westwards towards the Shannon.

A canal boat passes a cottage on the Leinster Aqueduct.

Paddle boarding is growing in popularity on the Barrow Line.

Chapter V

THE BARROW LINE: LOWTOWN

— TO —

ATHY

45km

Just beyond Robertstown are Lowtown and Lock 19, marking an important division between the main line of the Grand Canal, heading west towards Shannon Harbour, and a southerly branch known as the Grand Canal Barrow Line, which travels down through Rathangan and Monasterevin to Athy, there to merge with the Barrow River.

It's a good 45km from Lowtown down to Athy, but it's a fascinating walk through some lovely landscape and interesting

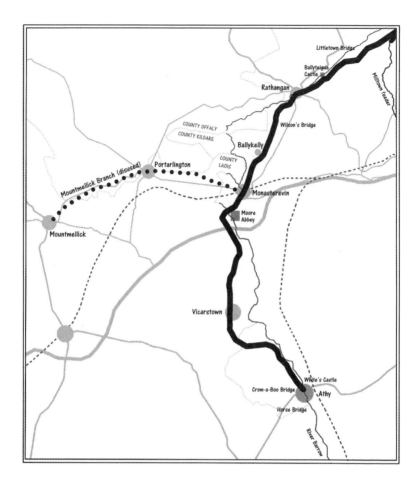

towns and bridges, which offer plenty of choice for breaking the route up into several sections over time.

From the beginning, when the canal was first thought of as a feasible project, this link to the south coast was considered of equal – if not more - importance than connecting to the Shannon on the west, since Waterford was then one of our largest ports, serving ships from all across the world. An efficient link between that harbour and Dublin was therefore much to be desired by commercial minds of the time, and work started on this branch in 1783, just four years after the canal had reached Robertstown.

Although the Barrow river does run close to the Grand Canal's main line here, its upper reaches were totally unsuitable for canalising, being too narrow, too varied in depth, and generally too difficult to tame into canal form. And so it was decided to build an entirely fresh stretch of canal. This would more or less follow the route of the main river down through Rathangan to Monasterevin, and there blend into it, forming one smooth link to the south. So great was the desire for this connection among the merchant minds of Dublin that, although it was found in the end that it was not feasible to meet the river at Monasterevin, and the canal had to continue to Athy, the Barrow Line was actually finished in the early 1790s, well ahead of the main line reaching the Shannon in 1804.

Two canals can be seen to be heading southwest here, not just one. The first, known now as the Old Barrow Line, and no longer open to boat traffic, is met at Fenton Bridge, while the second (formally known as the Barrow Line) is a very short distance beyond, at Lock 19.

The Old Barrow Line was constructed in the 1790s, with its own nineteenth lock some 2km down. It was used for some years, but around 1803, in the interests of economising on water supply, a newer branch was dug a little west of this, and the older declared out of use. However, canny bargemen soon took to using the older branch to get south, slipping through at night and avoiding the toll charges on the new canal. When this was discovered and reported to the directors in Dublin,

Milltown Bridge on the Barrow Line.

they took steps to close that loophole or bypass. Today only the newer, more westerly branch is open to boats on the Barrow Line at Lowtown. Walkers, however, can take the line of the older canal, and see where the two meet, further down at the old nineteenth lock.

About 1.5km down the Barrow Line from the junction with the main canal is Littletown Bridge, with a local pub, The Traveller's Rest, offering temptation to pause awhile. The Milltown Feeder canal comes in near here to keep the water levels up. It draws its supplies from freshwater springs at Pollardstown Fen, and these are claimed to be exceptionally clear and sparkling.

Another km or so and Skew Bridge comes into view, followed immediately by the old nineteenth lock, and then that meeting of the waters – the junction where the old and new Barrow lines come together to continue as one. There is a plaque to look out for here which gives the history of the old nineteenth. Many barges and other craft are moored along here, some permanently occupied, with a constant to and fro of boat residents moving along the towpaths, visiting each other or coming back to their craft with their shopping.

Ballyteigue Castle (or Ballyteague, spellings vary) shows up on the northwestern bank, followed by Ballyteigue Bridge. The castle is really a fortified house, dating from various building periods between the fourteenth and sixteenth centuries. That famous rebel, Silken Thomas, of the great Kildare Fitzgeralds, is reputed to have taken refuge here in 1535 after things did not go his way in the Kildare Rebellion. It didn't give the young Earl shelter for long, as he was captured and taken to the Tower of London in August of that year, later to be beheaded at Tyburn for treason to the English crown.

Skew Bridge at Ballyteigue, where the old and new Barrow Lines meet.

And in case you were wondering, it is said that he got the nickname Silken Thomas from the fact that he equipped his followers with silk fringes to their helmets. Probably made them easier to distinguish in a skirmish.

The twentieth and twenty-first locks of the Barrow Line come shortly after Ballyteigue Castle and its violent history are passed, and a further 3km brings the canal across the charming little Griffith Aqueduct, which crosses the River Slate here. Look over to the east and there, not 4km away as the raven flies, is the Hill of Allen, where Fionn MacCumhaill and his legendary followers, the Fianna, are said to have dwelt, and where his treasure may still lie buried. Unfortunately the hill is now being extensively quarried for useful stone, which has changed its original shape somewhat.

A noticeable folly still stands on top of the hill, however, built by a local landlord, Sir Gerard Aylmer in 1859. It took a lot of men and a lot of work, but at least he acknowledged their labour, inscribing their names on the eighty-three steps leading up to the viewing platform. An interesting find during the excavations and building work was a large coffin containing human bones. These remains were courteously re-interred at the time, but of course the legend has grown to attribute them to none other than the great Fionn himself.

Some 4km of pleasant strolling in gentle green countryside, and Glenaree Bridge and the twenty-second lock are in view. Beyond the bridge, the canal stretches along a high embankment until Rathangan is reached. Be sure to keep an eye open for unusual plants or flowers below the embankment. The creation of the canal over 200 years ago meant

Pottering along under a leafy canopy. A canal boat on the Barrow Line.

that all the inroads of later development left this landscape untouched, so that much of the flora that was once common all over Ireland can still be found here.

After about 4.5km, the old canalside warehouses of Rathangan are reached by the town's bridge, the twenty-third lock (which is a double) and Spencer Bridge. Rathangan has some fine Georgian houses that were built at the same time as the canal, but there has been a settlement here from far older times, as a venerable rath or ringfort on the edge of the town shows. The town gets its name from this Rath of Iomghán (c.600AD), which actually has the distinction of inspiring an eighth-century Irish poem:

> Once it was Bruidge's, it was Cathal's,
> It was Ard's, it was Ailill's.
> It was Conaing's, it was Cuiline's,
> And it was Maelduin's.
> The fort remains after each in his turn,
> And the kings asleep in the grounds.
>
> (Original author unknown; translation Kuno Meyer)

What would those lords of ancient Ireland have thought if their druids had shown them a vision of the future: a waterway crossing their kingdom, carrying ships crowded with people and goods from one side of the country to the other? Perhaps they come forth at the powerful times of year like Samhain and Bealtaine, gaze down thoughtfully on the canal, the locks, the bridges, and observe that these too in their turn have slipped into the past, into a gentle quietness.

Spencer Bridge and lock at Rathangan.

The novelist, cookery writer, playwright and journalist, Maura Laverty, was born and bred in Rathangan. Famed for *Kind Cooking*, a culinary bible first published in 1946, but dateless in its humorous practicality, she also wrote several novels. At least two of these (*Alone We Embark and Lift Up Your Gates*) achieved that cultural recognition so desired by Irish writers, of being banned in her own country. *Never No More: The Story of a Lost Village*, a semi-fictionalised account of her childhood, has been republished by Virago and is well worth reading for its accurate portrayal of a world that has now disappeared. Ms Laverty's plays for the Gate Theatre in Dublin, *Liffey Lane* and *Tolka Row*, were very successful in the 1950s, and from the latter came RTÉ's very first family drama series.

For younger readers, *The Cottage in the Bog* is a minor classic, with wonderful descriptions of rural life by the canal in the

1940s, spiced up with mystery, detective work, hidden treasure and hairsbreadth narrow escapes. It is currently out of print, but is one of those books that ought to be tracked down, read and kept to be handed on. Parents will enjoy it every bit as much as their children.

If you feel like a change from the towpath, you can explore Killinthomas Woods, about 2km north of Rathangan. It's a beautiful area of some 200 acres with easy signposted walks, ideal for the family and dog. In late spring/early summer, the bluebells here are a sight to behold. They even have their own Bluebells and Buskers festival in May. At any time of the year, though, it's a lovely place.

Some 7.5km divides Spencer Bridge and the twenty-third lock on the Barrow Line from Macartney's Bridge and the twenty-fourth lock near Ballykelly. In between are some

The seventh-century Rath of Iomghán at Rathangan.

interesting features to spot, as well as a spot of folklore to consider. Just beyond Wilson's Bridge (3km from Spencer Bridge) is a little aqueduct that carries the canal over Duke's Drain. To the east lies an old castle, around which legend has it that the Dead Coach is sometimes seen. This rather worrying coach appears when someone is near passing from this life. Its driver, wrapped in a many-caped greatcoat as the stage coach drivers of old, is headless, and his four or six black horses the same. Several people from Rathangan recorded their experiences of seeing the frightening apparition in earlier years.

(As a point of interest, should the Dead Coach ever be heard or seen approaching your own home, the most important thing to do is open all gates and doors, especially those that will give a clear route through. With luck, the coach driver will drive right on and pass out of sight. That is what the old received wisdom advises anyway. Might be useful to keep in mind.)

Umeras Bridge offers splendid views over the surrounding countryside and bogland, and is only a short distance from Umeras Peatlands Park, a new community initiative that aims to restore the natural balance of the bog in this region and develop it as a facility for exploration and nature discovery.

Just below Macartney's Bridge and the twenty-fourth lock, and right on the canal, lies the intriguingly named Church of Oak. This is in fact a new distillery, sited in the old Bally-kelly mills here, so that the place where grain brought in by barge was once ground is now using grain to create new and exciting whiskies. It is whispered that superstar Bono is one of the investors in this development. The original mill, rising to seven stories, was built in the early 1800s. The Grand Canal was used to send its products to Dublin and also onward to England and Scotland. It is a really good feeling to see old buildings repurposed to new commercial activity, echoing history while looking forward.

Hardly 3km now into Monasterevin, a historic town whose unusual number of bridges have, inevitably, given it the name of the Venice of Ireland. Granted by James I to Sir Adam Loftus in the early seventeenth century, it became the property of Lord Charles Moore, Earl of Drogheda, at the end of that century when he married into the Loftus family. The Moores were good landlords, improving the town and laying out new streets. They also built a spectacular home of their own, Moore Abbey.

Moore Abbey was the home of that legendary tenor, Count John McCormack, from 1925 to 1937, and saw many famous guests entertained there. McCormack recorded several of his albums in the Great Hall, and one of the scenes from his film *Song o' My Heart* was actually filmed in the grounds of Moore Abbey. It is now the Irish headquarters of the Sisters of Charity of Jesus and Mary, and known as the Muiriosa Foundation.

The poet Gerard Manley Hopkins stayed in Monasterevin on several occasions and spoke most affectionately of it, calling the river 'the burling Barrow brown'. There is an active Hopkins society there today.

But there is noisier history too. On 2 July 1903, the Gordon Bennett Cup came through its streets. This was the

Moore's dramatic drawbridge at Monasterevin.

first international motor race to be held in either Ireland or Great Britain, and as racing was by then illegal on British public roads, Ireland became the venue. The straightness of roads in Kildare made it a clear choice, and the 528km circuit, starting at Ballyshannon crossroads near Calverstown, encompassed Kilcullen, Kildare, Monasterevin, Stradbally, Athy, Castledermot and Carlow. It was won by the Belgian Camille Jenatzy, driving a Mercedes.

Another little-known fact: As a compliment to Ireland, the British team chose to race in a colour they christened Shamrock Green, which ever after became known as British Racing Green, that dark shade so beloved of the owners of vintage Bentleys. A bit too dark for a shamrock, as any Irish person will know, but it was a nice gesture.

Aqueduct over the River Barrow at Monasterevin.

The coming of the Grand Canal allowed the local distilling industry to flourish, especially the Cassidy family enterprise, which built its international fame on its whiskey and St Patrick Cross Pale Ale. Both were exported by canal, so the new project at Church of Oak is carrying on a long tradition.

The bridges everywhere are a sign of the waterway's presence too. Once you have passed under the main Dublin–Cork railway line, you come to the Drawbridge, where the main road crosses the waterway. This is the only lifting structure of its kind on the Grand Canal. At any time of day, you might hear a blaring siren warning traffic to stop and wait. The barriers go down and the bridge is lifted, allowing a boat through and on to the splendid 1826 aqueduct, carrying the canal over the River Barrow. The eagle-eyed may also spot the busy lock keeper, dashing from the drawbridge to the twenty-fifth lock at Moore Bridge on the southern edge of town, to open and shut the gates there too.

THE MOUNTMELLICK BRANCH

Just before the twenty-fifth lock, the now disused Mountmellick Canal can just be discerned, leading off to the right (assuming you are travelling south) or, more accurately, westwards. It has been mostly filled in, and much of the land sold off, so the only way to explore it is to drive the R420 into the neighbouring county of Laois (you've been in Kildare up to now), past medieval Lea Castle to Portarlington, and on to the town that in the nineteenth century was known as the Manchester of Ireland for its prosperous industries. Today, Mountmellick is a quiet backwater, but a lovely place to visit, with echoes of its past importance everywhere.

Thirteenth-century Lea Castle, almost hidden in the trees by the Barrow.

In fact, by the beginning of the nineteenth century, Mountmellick was extremely wealthy, with a very large population working in spinning and textile mills run by Quaker families, as well as in breweries and tanneries. As soon as the Barrow Line reached Monasterevin, therefore, it was not surprising that the leading businesses of Mountmellick began to see the considerable advantages of having a branch to their town, so that goods could more easily be transported in and out.

The work of digging began in 1827, and the canal was opened for business, both goods and passengers, in 1831. The route more or less followed the flood plain of the River Barrow over relatively flat ground, and the canal only required three locks to be constructed.

… A branch of the Grand Canal, which has been brought to the
town from Monastereven [sic] has greatly promoted its trade in
corn, butter, and general merchandise, which is rapidly increasing.

Samuel Lewis, *A Topographical Dictionary of Ireland*, 1837

It proved very popular with passengers, since it was considered
far smoother than coach travel, and indeed safer, as interruptions
or attacks were far less likely, and they were assured that the boats
in any case carried defensive weapons for their protection. On
arrival in Mountmellick, travellers could join a Bianconi carriage
for onward transport to Birr.

It was goods, particularly heavy goods, that kept the Mountmellick branch very busy, though. Timber, coal, hides, tar,
hardware and manure came down from Dublin, while malt,
flour and wheat travelled back up. Malt was one of the biggest
exports of the town, all of it going up to feed the ever-hungry
Guinness brewery at St James' Gate in Dubin.

The very first factory to extract sugar from beet was opened
at Mountmellick in 1851, with enough steam power to process
300 tons of the root vegetable a week. In 1876, Odlums opened
its mill at Portarlington, with its own wharf. By then the railway
had arrived, but the major milling company, still a byword today
for its legendary oatmeal, made full use of both methods of
transport. For canal work, Odlums had three of its own barges.

Russell Brothers sawmills also opened in Portarlington, but
much later, in 1914. Timber was shipped to the mills by the
canal and then travelled onward as the finished product to
Dublin, from where it was destined for the UK. It has been
claimed, and it is probably true, that wood from the Russell

Plaque on MacCartney's Bridge.

mill was used to make those ever-flying bobbins for the cotton mills of Lancashire.

Passenger traffic ended with the coming of the railways, and eventually road vehicles spelt the end for the Mountmellick Canal. The last load of malt for Dublin left in 1940. Bill Lawlor, son of Grand Canal Company agent John Lawlor, was born in the agent's house in Mountmellick, where he still lives today. He is a mine of information about the malt shipments and everything else to do with the canal.

There was 12 stone in every one of those bags of malt, you'd have nine or ten carts carrying eight bags at a time. They would be loaded onto the boat there off the quay. The last of those [barges] went out in March 1940. Oh, we had more boats coming in after that one, with other goods, but that particular job was over. The malt shipments were finished.

Grain barges from Dublin to Odlums Mill kept the section to Portarlington open a little longer, but by the 1950s, even the Odlums boats were no longer in use. The Mountmellick canal was finally closed officially in 1960. Since then, much has been filled in, roads have been constructed along stretches, and nature has taken over the rest. In Mountmellick itself, about the only visible evidence that it was ever there can be found down at the agent's house where Bill Lawlor lives, and a pub close by that bears the name The Canal End. The canal basin used to be behind the Lawlor home, but it too has been filled in to provide space for a housing estate. Yet in the town itself, feelings still run high. 'It was the worst thing in the world, the closing of our canal,' said the energetic proprietor of a local newsagents to a chorus of assent from her customers. 'Look what an advantage it would be today, with all that traffic on the roads! They should never have done it.'

It's worth a side trip by car to see Mountmellick, to admire the still elegant remains of its fine buildings, to read the informative signboards telling of its past glories, and perhaps to take coffee in the square while you imagine just how crowded and busy it must have been in the days when it was 'the Manchester of Ireland'.

Back to the Barrow Line

From Monasterevin it is about 6km to Fisherstown Bridge, whose name suggests the occupations of earlier communities here. On the way, there is another little aqueduct over a small river (where, incidentally, you cross over from Kildare into Laois), and then the towpath ducks under the roaring M7 motorway to resume its peaceful way south. Another 5.5km to Vicarstown, passing yet another little aqueduct (the navvies must have shaken their heads and sighed wearily when they met each little tributary river and realised that yet more stonework would be needed rather than the regular digging), and then Courtwood Bridge, followed by Grattan Aqueduct. From here, it's only about 2.5km to Vicarstown Bridge.

A direct rendering from the Irish, *Baile an Bhiocáire* (meaning 'town of the vicar'), Vicarstown sits at the junction where the R427 crosses the canal. Though seemingly in the middle of

Camac Aqueduct over the Stradbally River on the Barrow Line.

nowhere, it sustains a good big pub, and at weekends enthusiastic groups of paddleboarders make the energetic journey up and down from Athy or Monasterevin to foregather here and congratulate each other on their long water trek.

The Camac aqueduct comes next, and Ballymanus Bridge, beyond which the canal pops back into Co. Kildare and turns eastwards towards Milltown Bridge (6km from Vicarstown). From here it is just 5km to Athy and the end of the Barrow Line canal.

ATHY

There was a settlement here on the strategically important crossing of the Barrow from Anglo-Norman times. Later it came into the lordship of the Fitzgeralds, earls of Kildare, who built most of the town and held it for several centuries. Athy found itself inconveniently trapped between warring parties at the time of Royalists, Parliamentarians and Confederates, and suffered much damage. Even the all-important medieval bridge was destroyed. The current one, rejoicing in the name of the Crom-a-Boo, dates from 1796.

The town was bombarded by cannon fire many times and the Dominican Monastery, the local castles and the town's bridge (dating from 1417) all succumbed to the destructive forces of the cannonball. The current bridge, the Crom-a-Boo Bridge, was built in 1796, when the Barrow Line of the Grand Canal was beginning to spread industry and prosperity once more.

Athy, being on the very edge of the Pale, was always a garrison town, owing its allegiance to the English crown, and English soldiers were billeted here for centuries. The splendid courthouse and corn exchange remind one more of an English market town than a typical Irish one. There is a bronze statue here of Ernest Shackleton, standing with folded arms, surveying the Heritage Centre, which holds a permanent display dedicated to him. The Antarctic explorer was born at Kilkea, near Athy, in 1874.

Although regarded in the capital as a defensive outpost of the Pale, Athy was a good distance from Dublin, and until the canal came, few must have visited this outpost. Patrick Kavanagh reflects that view of the town as remote and little-known in his famous poem, 'Lines Written on a Seat on the Grand Canal, Dublin':

> And look! a barge comes bringing from Athy
> And other far-flung towns mythologies.

One of the most striking sights is White's Castle, a sixteenth-century tower house standing right at the entrance to the main bridge. It is on the site of an earlier castle dating from 1417 and built by Sir John Talbot, then Viceroy of Ireland, to protect this strategic site. Huge and dominating, it effortlessly commands the town's narrow streets and waterways. As it was intended to do.

Those narrow streets, almost medieval in their layout, can often lead to traffic jams and delays. On the other hand, one of Athy's most charming aspects is the plethora of little local shops, old traditional names over their doors, doing business as they have done for generations. Few of the big international commercial giants can be found in Athy, but if you're looking for a local grocer, a shoe shop where they greet you

White's Castle and Crom-a-Boo Bridge at Athy.

in friendly manner, a butcher who will go out of his way to advise on the best cut, little clothes emporiums that you thought had disappeared in today's over-modernised world, then you will delight in exploring Athy.

The best sight is still to come, though. Downstream of Crom-a-Boo Bridge, a narrower, lighter span can be discerned casting itself across the water. This is the delightfully single-lane, cobbled Horse Bridge, where the Barrow Line of the Grand Canal finally comes to meet the strongly flowing river from which it takes its name.

Lock gates give access to the main waterway, which from here on would take goods downstream to join its sister, the Nore. They then go on together to Waterford. Similarly, boats brought upriver, laden with products destined for Dublin or elsewhere along the main line of the canal, would enter the lock system and start on their journey north to Lowtown.

Opposite: Where the Barrow Line on the left meets its parent river: Lock 28 and Horse Bridge at Athy.
Above: The old courthouse in Athy.

It is quite a sight to see canal meet natural waterway at this point, while upriver, White's Castle broods and thinks its own thoughts about travel and history.

We have reached the end of the Barrow Line. Of course, there is another long distance walk onward from here, all along the river and down to the south coast, but that is not the province of this book. We head back to the main line of the Grand Canal where we left it at Robertstown.

Binns Bridge at Robertstown.

Chapter VI

ROBERTSTOWN

── TO ──

EDENDERRY

c.22km

This next is a wonderfully historic stretch of the Grand Canal, with stories in every kilometre of the towpath. It's a simple one to break up into walkable sections too (although easy enough to do in one cycling trip).

When leaving Robertstown, don't forget to look back as you pass under Binns Bridge, to see the old hotel framed by the arch. It's a lovely sight now, and must have been even more welcome to the eyes of weary travellers yearning for a comfortable bed and good food before continuing their journey.

Of course, passengers on the canal boats didn't have to wait to reach one of the company's hotels to break their

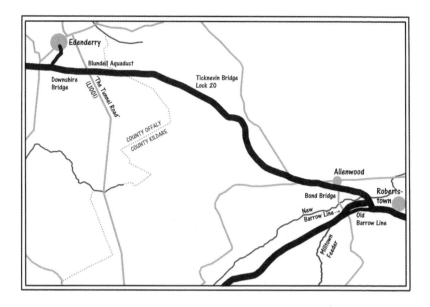

fast. Food was provided on board for all who wanted it (and could pay). Dinner for first-class passengers cost two shillings a head, with the addition of a pint of wine almost doubling that. Second-class travellers could obtain dinner at the somewhat lower rate of one shilling and threepence a head, but wine wasn't allowed to these lesser mortals: they could only purchase cider or porter, at ten pence or five pence respectively, to accompany their meal. Breakfast (with eggs, plural) in the superior section of the boat cost a shilling and threepence, while in the lesser cabin it was just tenpence (but with only one egg).

Some travellers found the dining facilities satisfactory: Sir John Carr commented:

> We had an excellent dinner on board, consisting of a leg of boiled mutton, a turkey, ham, vegetables and porter, and a pint of wine each, at four shillings and ten pence a head.
>
> *A Stranger in Ireland*, 1805

Others were less than courteous about the food supplied, notably Antony Trollope, who described

> the eternal half-boiled leg of mutton, floating in a bloody sea of grease and gravy, which always comes on the table three hours after the departure from Porto Bello.
>
> *The Kellys and the O'Kellys*, 1848

An anonymous correspondent of the *Dublin Evening Packet and Correspondent* in the summer of 1831, describing a recent trip on the Grand Canal, made some amused observations on the dining arrangements:

> Dinner now made its appearance, 'smoking on the board.' A leg of mutton ushered in the train, gracefully leading after it chickens and bacon, and an immense piece of boiled beef and cabbage.

Once a welcome sight for canal travellers, the old hotel at Robertstown.

'Where is my porta, gul?' said a fat-faced, ruddy-visaged gentleman, one of our Reverences from the College. 'Where is my porta that I paid for?' 'The Captain is drawing the cork, Sir,' said the smiling Hebe; you shall have the porter directly.' 'I declare I'm chouking with thurst; till the Kiptin to send me in my bautle, and I'll draw the cork myself. The best way to drive a cork in a hurry, gentlemen, is to push it down.'

'Sir, I'd throuble you for another shliver of mouton,' asked our small grocer from Tuam; 'it ates remarkably well and thick.' 'The pleasure of a glass of wine, ma'am, with you, if you plaise. Phoo, this is nothing but slow water; it's a grate shame for Mister Blake not to give better wine in the boat;' and so

We eat, and drank, and wined, and then

We wined, and drank, and eat again.

Musing on the dining habits of yesteryear will bring you along the 1.5km easy stroll from Binns Bridge to Fenton Bridge and the nineteenth lock at Lowtown. This was, for many years, one of the busiest places anywhere along the canal, both at the construction stage and during its time as a transport hub. That is because the Barrow Line branches off southwest here, to join up with the River Barrow much further down at Athy, and thus link the Grand Canal with Waterford. In the late eighteenth century, this was considered a connection of the highest importance. All the information on this branch line will be found in the preceding chapter.

As well as marking the branching off south of the Barrow Line, the nineteenth lock marks the start of what is known as the Summit Level, a long stretch of (fairly) even landscape across the central boglands. The canal here was supplied with water from two feeders: the Milltown, which drew from a source at Pollardstown Fen, and the Blackwood, from a reservoir dug at Foranfan.

Some 1.8km further along the towpath comes Bond Bridge and the R415, which will take you north to the village of Allenwood, developed in the nineteenth century as a coaching stop on the old road to Edenderry; or south through Derrymullen and Littletown to Harberton Bridge on the Barrow Line. That circuit in itself might make an interesting walk – about 4.5km from Fenton Bridge, out one way, back the other.

Less than 1.5km beyond this is Shee Bridge, crossed by the R403, after which the canal curves to the northwest. A further 3km along, there is an interesting Bord na Móna lifting bridge,

A boat passes under the Bord na Móna lifting bridge.

used to service the little bog railway that carried turf from cutting points to storage areas for onward transmission. It is not much used these days, but when it was, one wonders who had right of way, the boat or the train? Did steam give way to sail, so to speak, as on the high seas?

Hamilton's Bridge is 2.5km further on. At this point, you are 24 Irish miles (49km) from Dublin. (Okay, okay, about 30.5 English miles, that satisfy you?) Now the canal turns somewhat more westerly again near Abbeylough Bridge, to reach Ticknevin Bridge and the twentieth lock after a further 4.2km.

The village of Derrinturn, about 2.5km north of the canal at Ticknevin Bridge, carries old history in its name, being translated as 'oak wood of the furnace'. Clearly smelting or charcoal burning was carried on here in earlier times, although no traces remain today. It's a useful place to pause, though, if you are running short of supplies.

From the twentieth lock on is the longest stretch of the Grand Canal without a single lock: some 30km across the spreading bogland, right through to Ballycommon and the twenty-first. This was one of those regions where the work was even more arduous than usual; problems were constantly faced in dealing with the uncooperative bogland. The navvies, not to mention the engineers, must have despaired at times of ever succeeding in digging the canal, lining it with clay and filling it with water. So many times the banks collapsed, the water drained away. No wonder it took so long to build.

Today, a stretch of open bogland with its myriad wild flowers and rare water plants, butterflies, hares and rabbits is regarded as a wonderful place for relaxation and rediscovery

A well-used mooring ring of yesteryear at the Blundell Aqueduct.

of nature's beauty. It was not always regarded thus. The canal creators, as we have seen, saw it as one of the great challenges to their work, which would defeat them at every stage if it could. To the travellers by boat, it was equally unattractive, as evidenced by the description by another unnamed gentleman in the *Dublin Penny Journal* of 19 September 1835:

The Grand Canal from Dublin to Ballinasloe passes through the middle of the Bog of Allen. Being desirous of seeing a spot, with which so many interesting events in the history of Ireland are connected, I availed myself, in the autumn of 1834, of the circumstance of having some business which required my presence in the County of Galway, to go there by the Canal packet …

For the first twenty miles or so, this traveller was delighted with the 'rich and varied' scenery encountered. But then, all changed when:

… you find yourself upon the Bog of Allen. Words cannot describe the overwhelming sensations that are produced by the contrast in the aspect of the scene of dreariness and desolation that now presents itself, and every where surrounds you. To comprehend them it must be seen. Imagine yourself – or, as it was with me, that you had gone down for a couple of hours to the cabin, and then returned upon deck – imagine yourself, then, suddenly transported from the delightful scenes I have described, to a wild dreary waste, covered with patches of gorse and dingy brown heath, alternating with the black surface of the bog, or with some slimy morass; and no other marks of inhabitation or of cultivation, save here and there an insulated hovel, its roof barely raised above the soil, in which it appears to be, and not infrequently is, imbedded …

So struck was this gentleman with the apparent poverty of the inhabitants of these huts that he enquired of a doctor travelling on the same boat if they were not perpetually ailing and suffering.

'Nothing of the sort, I assure you,' he replied; 'they in general enjoy admirable health; and I know of no complaint to which they are particularly liable, except,' he added, laughing, 'it be to that of hunger occasionally.'

'To what causes, then do you ascribe their exemption from the diseases incident to such situations?'

'Indeed, I know of no other, unless it be the antiseptic quality of our bogs.'

It is no more than 5km from the twentieth lock to another engineering marvel, the Blundell Aqueduct, where the canal sails happily over the road, and those on the towpath can look down on cars and lorries as they have, perforce, to slow down from their usual rapid speed, and negotiate a sharp turn in the near-dark of what is locally known as The Tunnel.

The aqueduct was built in 1793 to carry the canal over the Edenderry to Rathangan Road. Partly funded by the local landlord, it was, of course, named after him, as so many bridges were named after members of the Grand Canal Company.

Road below, canal above! The Blundell Aqueduct.

This sort of thing was a recognition of your importance and thus much pursued by those who considered themselves worthy of the accolade.

The aqueduct is unusual in that it is the only structure in Offaly to carry a canal over a road. Usually they bring it dry shod (so to speak) over a minor river or stream, although the Leinster Aqueduct, further back near Sallins, is noteworthy for bridging the Liffey itself (admittedly in its upper reaches) and a considerable valley, both challenges enough.

Less than 2km now to the delightfully narrow little Down-shire Bridge (designed for horses and individual people, not vehicles), which marks the branch line up to Edenderry. Take the time to stroll over it, remembering the days when five-lane motorways were not only unimaginable, but unnecessary. One horse, one man, what more space do you need?

Enough for one day? Turn aside and stroll a relaxing 1km up the greenway which leads you into Edenderry. It is a nice little market town with the raised basin of the canal form-ing quite a dramatic feature at its centre. Climbing the steps to the edge of the basin, where barges moored and goods were weighed for onward transport, you can only imagine the hard labour it must have taken to build that massive emplacement. Historically, though, it was definitely consid-ered worth it, for the improvement in commerce it would bring to the town.

Standing on a hill just to the north of the town is Blundell Castle, now in ruins, but still most effective on its height. The current structure dates from around the thirteenth century. It was probably built on the site of an earlier, Norman castle built by the de Berminghams, who had been granted the land by Strongbow. This of course started prolonged feuding with the O'Connors, the hereditary owners of this region.

However, as so often happened, the de Berminghams and the O'Connors then joined together against the newer English threats. The *Annals of Connacht* record that the castle was attacked and pulled down by John Talbot, then Lord Lieutenant of Ireland, in 1416. The *Annals of Ulster*, however, state firmly that in 1417, 'The castle of Edan-daire in Offaly was broken down by Foreigners.' The apparent contradiction can probably be explained by the fact that to Irish eyes at the time, an English lord was a foreigner.

By the sixteenth century, though, the lands had been granted by Queen Elizabeth I to the planter family of Colley or Cowley, as part of her plans to subdue the 'wild Irish' by a comprehensive process of plantation with English settlers.

Blundell Castle at Edenderry.

The Colleys gave their name to the barony of Coolestown, in which Edenderry is situated. Of interest to treasure hunters is the belief that there are silver mines located on the hill near the castle, and that might explain why Welsh miners were brought in at some point during the ownership of the Colleys. Presumably they were hoping to strike it rich, but Ireland's silver (and indeed gold) mines have never been rich producers, and would not have justified the considerable expense involved in extracting the ore.

In the 1650s, the castle passed into the hands of George Blundell, who married Sarah Colley. The couple received unwelcome notoriety in 1674, when their three sons were accused of murdering the son of the Catholic peer, Lord Tara. They were, however, subsequently acquitted by Charles II.

In 1691, though, came the eventual downfall of Blundell Castle. The family had sided with the Williamites against the Jacobites, and the Jacobite forces – oddly enough, under the command of Lt. Col. O'Connor - destroyed both the castle and the town. The castle was never occupied again and was left to its memories. Both Sarah and one of her sons, Francis, are buried in Edenderry, and local legend holds that Blundell Castle is haunted by Sarah's ghost to this day.

The original Irish name of the town, *Eadan Doire*, or Hill of the Oak Wood, was changed to Coolestown during that family's ownership. In later centuries, however, it was returned to its delightfully descriptive Irish name.

When the Grand Canal was under construction in the late eighteenth century, two Blundell sisters, descendants of Sarah and George, who now lived in the town rather than the ruined castle, firmly opposed local proposals that it should have a linking branch thereto. Once the Marquess of Downshire inherited, though, he very quickly reversed that decision, and actually paid out of his own pocket the cost of the project (estimated at between £690 and £1000 at the time). The Edenderry branch was completed and functioning in 1802.

Incidentally, the Marquess, who seemed extremely determined to raise the standard of living in the town, also took over a small neighbouring village called Glann. She incorporated it into Edenderry, improved its tenement buildings, added a stretch of ground to each for the purpose of growing food, and let them out to suitable tenants at a nominal rent of one shilling a year.

There had been a thriving industry in woollen cloth manufacturing here since the early eighteenth century, employing around a thousand local people, as well as a tannery and a brewery. The convenience of a canal right on their doorstep meant that goods could be transported to Dublin or the Shannon very efficiently.

Edenderry suffered like so many other Irish towns during the Famine. An advertisement for the local workhouse in 1848 invited tenders to supply a very wide range of necessities for its unfortunate inmates, including:

50 yds Galway Flannel ... 100 yds Blue Calico for infants' frocks ... 4 stones yarn for Knitting ... 2 gross Iron Spoons ... 100 Chambers ... plus spades, shovels, and stone hammers.

General Advertiser, 30 September 1848

Perhaps surprisingly, at the dawn of the twentieth century, two motor car manufacturers with claims to fame were based here in Edenderry, when you might reasonably have expected them to pop up in our capital city. William Corrigan, a local garage owner, is credited with inventing a 4½hp car in 1902, and a model created by the Alesbury brothers was exhibited at the 1907 Dublin Motor Show.

Built of wood, and powered by an 8/10hp Stevens engine, the Alesbury had solid tyres (Mr Dunlop's new-fangled pneumatic invention clearly holding no attraction for its creators). Manufacture of the Alesbury, however, lasted only until 1908. It would be nice to know if there are any still in existence. (The Thomas Cubitt Engineering Company in the UK appears to claim ownership of a rare vehicle dating from the 1920s,

Narrow little Downshire Bridge and the branch line up to Edenderry on the left.

Overgrown but still popular: the Edenderry Branch.

called the Aylesbury, and says there are only about seven left in the world today, but they do not acknowledge the invention by the Alesbury brothers at Edenderry in the earlier part of the century. Still something to be teased out there.)

Towns like Edenderry are little noticed by tourism, since they are in the central heartlands rather than in the more obvious coastal locations, but they encapsulate in their very energy the essence of old-world Ireland, where everybody knows everybody else, and local shops still bear the same names they did generations ago. It is a good experience to stroll around a place like this and see how relaxed and peaceful life can still be outside the maelstrom of our principal cities. There is little doubt that Edenderry owed much of its prosperity and growth to its link with that new and exciting commercial artery and great opportunity, the Grand Canal.

The canal basin in the centre of Edenderry.

Above: Colgan's Bridge, near Edenderry.

Below: Time-worn steps at Colgan's Bridge.

Chapter VII

ƐDENDERRY

── TO ──

ͲULLAMORE

c.35km

It's a good long stretch undeniably between Edenderry and Tullamore, but there are plenty of options to break it up into sections to be walked at different times to suit you. For example, pick-ups could be arranged at Trimblestown or Rhode bridges, or even at Daingean (*c*.20km).

An easy 1km leads down from Edenderry Harbour to the main line of the Grand Canal at Downshire Bridge, where a right turn puts you on the path for Daingean and Tullamore. Next comes a flurry of those lovely little humpbacked bridges – Colgan, Georges, and Rathmore – and one can only wonder

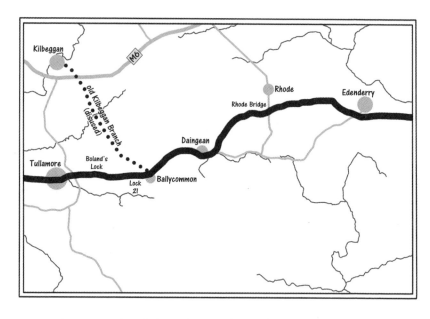

at the strength of those late-eighteenth-century structures, seeming today to cope easily with constant heavy traffic (even if large trucks and lorries have to take some care negotiating the sharp bends and humps). See if you can spot the worn old stone steps leading up from the towpath to the road at Colgan's Bridge. Residents around here have a long connection with the canal, counting generations of workers and bargemen in their families.

About 1.5km beyond this trio of crossings, after the canal curves northwest again, is Cartland Bridge, and 2km further on, as the waterway resumes its westward route, Trimblestown Bridge. These little bridges are a handy way to track your journey, although sometimes it's a jolt to see a heavy truck grinding in low gears overhead, as between those crossing points you are truly in the countryside, in an older, more peacefully slow world.

4.5km beyond Trimblestown is Rhode Bridge, which could be seen as the exact opposite to Edenderry. Instead of having a branch going right up into the town, goods for the small village of Rhode (2km to the north) were simply offloaded on to the canal bank, and men with horses and carts came down to collect them and carry them to their final destination. Imagine a stressed storekeeper waiting for deliveries from Dublin, wondering if his order was on the canal bank yet, and urging the cart driver to get down there at all possible speed? *'I have customers waiting!'*

Since the village stands on high ground, surrounded on all sides by the Bog of Allen, cut and dried turf would also have been carted down and loaded on to barges here at the bridge, for onward transmission to the capital where the need for fuel was never-ending.

A further kilometre, and Toberdaly Bridge comes into view, with the wind farm at Mount Lucas visible to the south. Next, a less traditional but very interesting structure, one of Bord Na Móna's lifting bridges, which allows a little bog train to run right across the flat landscape, trundling over the canal on its way. When not in use, the bridge lifts high on either side, allowing water traffic to pass by. It's a surprisingly peaceful place to stop and look at the worn boards and slightly rusty rails, while listening to a lark singing above the heather. An area near here is called Esker Beg, reminding us of the importance of eskers, or hard ridgeways of rock, for safe crossing of a dangerous boggy region in older times.

Heading southwest past Killeen Bridge, the canal swings direct west to take you into Daingean, no more than 4km from

Molesworth Bridge and quay at Daingean.

the lifting bridge. This was formerly a place of great importance as Philipstown, but is now a rather sleepy little village. Founded under Queen Mary, it was named for her husband, Philip of Spain, and was for a long time the county town of Offaly. The growing importance of Tullamore further to the west (principally due to its being the terminus of the Grand Canal for many years) eventually caused the seat of local government to be shifted there. Several rather grand structures still stand in Daingean as evidence of those earlier days – for example, the Courthouse on the main street.

There is a splendid old canal storehouse by Molesworth Bridge in the town too, recollecting all the goods and grain, animals and foodstuffs, that were brought here to be carried east or west and across the water. High above the towpath stands the uncompromising wall of an early fort, later St Conleth's reformatory school, and now a blameless joinery.

The early-nineteenth-century courthouse at Daingean.

A somewhat unusual sight is a traditional set of wooden stocks placed on the canal bank below that wall. This was more of an old English tradition, whereby those who had misbehaved would be locked into the stocks, so that local residents could insult them and throw rotten vegetables or eggs if they so wished.

Another Bord Na Móna bridge crosses the canal about 3km west of Daingean. This is a modern one, triple-arched and fixed, but allowing good clearance for passing boats. Now hurry on, because there is food for both body and mind waiting at Ballycommon Bridge, another 3km further along.

Ballycommon House has been looking after canal travellers for generations, first as a pub, then as a café, and now with holiday apartments attached. It is likely of course that there was an ale house of sorts here since the canal was built in the late eighteenth century. Gerry and Maria McGrath

Ballycommon House and Bridge.

Poppies bloom where the Kilbeggan branch leaves the main line at Ballycommon.

took over from Maria's uncle in 1984, and now son Kevin and his partner Aoife manage the temptingly named Ballycommon Bakehouse.

It's not just the coffee and freshly baked cakes, but the history you hear from Gerry that make this a must as a stopping point. Give it an hour or two and listen to the tales he tells, the old stories of early days, even to the actual digging of the canal in the late eighteenth century. Lore passed down from father to son over the generations.

Oh, it took them a long time to dig the bogland section – many years. It's the longest straight and level stretch on the whole canal – more than 30km from the twentieth lock at Ticknevin to the twenty-first just beyond here. People who had a horse and cart would bring loads of marl [clay] for making the bottom secure and waterproof. Then they would turn a flock of sheep into the trough to trample down the clay and make it firm.

Now, that bit about the sheep is fascinating factual detail that you wouldn't find in the history books. You could listen to Gerry all day, and envisage that huge army of labourers at their exhausting work, week after week, month after month, year after year, advancing so heartbreakingly slowly.

But the towpath beckons you on, and a short way beyond Ballycommon Bridge, after a gentle curve, stands the very building where barge horses were stabled and changed over. It has been adapted over the years of course, but you can see where the tired equines would have been led in through a large door at ground level, while above were stored the hay, oats and straw for their use.

Just beyond the former stabling, the delightfully narrow Campbell's Bridge (clearly constructed for horse traffic, not motor vehicles) marks the entrance to the Kilbeggan Branch canal, disused and overgrown, although a path has now been put in place to reconnect that town with the main line of the canal. It's worth taking a side trip up there (a good walk at near enough 13km, but you could drive round by road on another occasion), to see the oldest licensed distillery in Ireland, established in 1757.

Kilbeggan whiskey was shipped down the branch line and sent onwards to Dublin and the Shannon by water. Although the distillery saw bad times, and was eventually forced to close its doors in 1958, a strong sense of community ensured that the licence never lapsed, and Kilbeggan Distillery reopened in 1987. Today it is a thriving business and you could take the opportunity to taste the product while enjoying a tour of the historic buildings.

After a level run of more than 30km from the twentieth lock at Ticknevin Bridge, the twenty-first is reached just beyond Campbell's Bridge. From here on, there is a fairly rapid succession of locks until the twenty-sixth at Tullamore, reflecting the drop in ground levels between this high point and the considerably lower one at that town. The remains of an original Grand Canal lock keeper's cottage can still be seen by the twenty-first, next to a more modern one.

About 1.5km along the towpath from where the old Kilbeggan line branches off, come Lock 22 and Cappyroe Bridge. It's about half that again to the twenty-third, where you might well sight the local rowing club training hard on the 3km between here and the twenty-fourth. No need for you to make such an effort, though – just enjoy watching them while you stroll along the quiet canal bank at your own pace.

Charleville Castle near Tullamore.

There's hardly time to catch your breath between the twenty-fourth and twenty-fifth locks, since there is only a bare 600m between them. The bridge at the twenty-fifth has a plaque identifying it as Digby, which might cause confusion to those tracking their route carefully, as the sixteenth lock, way back at Kilcock in Kildare, is also known by this name. Perhaps one of the directors of the Grand Canal Company felt he was entitled to be remembered by more than one stone structure crossing this great waterway. Anyway, it is also known locally as Cappincur, after the local townland, so take your pick.

Now we are nearly into Tullamore, with less than 1km to the twenty-sixth or Boland's Lock, where there is a delightful example of architectural fancy in the shape of the two-storey, oval lock keeper's cottage. This one is certainly worth a picture or two. In summer months, it is open as a visitor centre. And if you keep your eyes open, you will spot Bye-Trader Boat 112B, also known as Terrapin, now permanently on dry land, just beyond the cottage and lock. Terrapin once worked as horse-drawn barge No. 21. Today it lies quietly amid the encroaching greenery, dreaming of long trips across the Irish countryside laden with cargoes in its younger days.

Soon the N52 ring road, with its busy traffic rushing across the bridge above the towpath, reminds us that the town of Tullamore is close by. Bury Bridge comes into view and the short side canal leading into Tullamore Harbour, where for six years (1798 to 1804), the Grand Canal ended. It took the directors a long time and a lot of wrangling before the best route onward to the Shannon was decided on. In the meantime, the town made the most of being the canal's terminus.

Kilbeggan Distillery, still thriving today.

Rest awhile in Tullamore, where the twenty-seventh and twenty-eighth locks as well as several bridges interpose on the canal's peaceful meandering. A splendid sight by the main bridge into the town is the old Tullamore Dew distillery. Now transformed into the Offaly History Centre, here local events across the centuries as well as family records and ancestors can be traced.

The famous distillery that once occupied this building (it's now on a greenfield site on the ring road outside the town, and you can take tours of its workings) was founded in the early 1800s by a local man, Michael Molloy. His nephew, Bernard Daly, inherited the distillery in the 1840s, and in the 1870s or early 1880s appointed Daniel E Williams as the general manager. And therein lies a small piece of distilling history.

Williams, born in 1848, came to work in Tullamore from Mountmellick (remember Mountmellick, a branch line from the Barrow Line, now, alas, disused and overgrown? You will find it in Chapter V). First just a mill-hand, the young man worked early and late, and eventually became overall manager of the distillery. In the 1890s, he created a new brand and used his own initials, D.E.W., to christen it: Tullamore Dew. The name caught on, was used in innumerable advertising slogans – 'Give Every Man His Dew' is still familiar – and the whiskey has proved popular across the world ever since.

The Tullamore distillery took full advantage of the Grand Canal's coming, having its own quayside and jetty built to ensure that the barrels of precious liquid could be transported down and loaded safely for their onward journeys to Dublin or Limerick (or indeed anywhere along the route that relished the unique flavour of their product). You can see it clearly from the canal towpath or from one of the foot bridges that crisscross it here.

The town has hotels, cafes, pubs and restaurants in plenty, so it is a good place to stay overnight. It was the Grand Canal indeed that made this town grow into the busy centre it is today. Back in the eighteenth century, it was a small place, its greatest claim to fame being a major fire caused by the explosion of a hot air balloon in 1785. No fatalities resulted, fortunately, but many thatched cottages were destroyed, and the event is remembered to this day in the town's crest, which shows a phoenix rising from the ashes, as Tullamore itself did.

The coming of the canal in 1798 resulted in steady growth and prosperity, which is probably why an 1832 act of parliament transferred county town status here from the previous holder, Philipstown (later Daingean). A magnificent hotel

The short branch under Bury Bridge, leading to the old harbour at Tullamore.

was built (now alas demolished) and passengers with deep enough purses could stay the night in relative comfort. It was not always possible to go straight from an arriving boat to a departing one leaving for your final destination and often an overnight stay was unavoidable.

The *Kerry Evening Post* of 23 December 1840 had a very definite bone to pick with that same hotel:

> Various complaints have reached us on account of the want of accommodation for passengers stopping at Tullamore from the packet-boats which arrive there at three o'clock each morning. The Company has a hotel, but they might as well be without one. The person in charge of it will not admit a traveller at night,

An aerial view showing the main line of the canal on the right, Bury Bridge is at bottom left, and the short link leading up to a right turn into the old harbour.

no matter what may be the state of the weather. One gentleman, who we can name, arrived in Tullamore at the hour mentioned, some few days back – the morning being most inclement, and the only place of shelter open to him was a stable, wherein he was compelled to stand shivering for some hours. His only alternative was the street, which was black as pitch. His suffering from cold was very intense. It is not our business to quarrel with the Canal Directors on account of any sum they choose to fix on for a rent; but on the part of the public, we do insist that they are bound to keep a servant in the hotel, and to afford accommodation for travellers until they shall find a tenant to their wishes. Leaving travellers exposed to the severity of the weather at this season of the year argues a want of feeling and a neglect of public duty in the Directors of the Grand Canal Company, which is highly reprehensible.

Perhaps this explains the advertisement taken out in 1842:

Grand Canal Hotel Tullamoore (sic) Formerly conducted by Mr. A. Morgan.

The present proprietor, B. Purcell, begs leave to inform the Public that this Hotel has been lately fitted up in the most respectable style for the reception of Travellers, to whom suitable and comfortable accommodation is offered on as moderate terms as in any similar establishment … Private families can be accommodated with separate apartments. Gentlemen resorting to it during the Assizes will be carried to and from the Court House free of Charge.

Dublin University Magazine, 1842

During the tragic years of the Famine in the late 1840s, the Grand Canal hotel at Tullamore was pressed into service as a grim auxiliary workhouse, capable, the authorities claimed, of containing 300 paupers. Not exactly the career its builders had envisaged for it, but those were cruelly harsh times in Ireland.

In earlier days, the better connected travellers might pass the time by visiting Charleville Castle, 3km south of the town. It is something anyone passing this way should do today. Dating from the early nineteenth century, the castle is set deep in one of our most ancient oak woods, once (it is said) the ritual meeting place of druids.

The castle itself is a wonderful neo-Gothic structure, but those who love nature will want above all to see the majestic King Oak, which has stood in these grounds for over 400 years and was Ireland's entry for European Tree of the Year back in 2013. Just to stand beneath its heavy boughs and look up into those far-reaching branches is to wonder how much of history it has seen, taken in and kept to itself over the centuries. Pay your respects to this great legend, and honour its presence in today's frantic world. You will find your mind returning to it as you relax and rest that evening in the friendly surrounds of Tullamore.

Opposite: Tullamore Harbour today, once a hive of activity.

Boland's lock keeper's house near Tullamore.

Keep your eyes
open and you just
might spot a brown
hare by the canal.

ʈULLAMORE

—— TO ——

ʈURRAUN

c.18km

This is perhaps the most scenically beautiful and peaceful section of the Grand Canal, stretching across the legendary bogland that forms the heart of this country. Heather and flowers, butterflies and shy wild animals abound, since the land here has lain largely unchanged since the navvies first wielded their spades centuries ago, to dig the endless trench that became the first long-distance waterway from east to west.

Strolling or cycling here, you really can forget the worries of the world, the clamouring headlines, the stresses of the city,

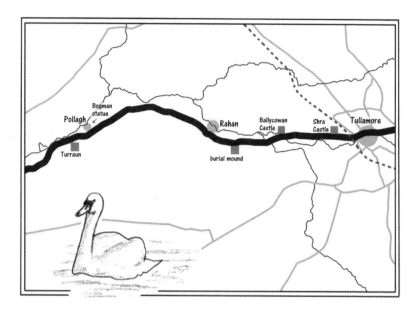

and instead recover some of that tranquillity, the peace of mind that comes when you are alone with nature and a gentle breeze is blowing overhead. No roads, no noisy traffic, no reminders of the modern day (unless you count a jet trail far away overhead, but why not admire the clouds through which it passes instead?). A rustle of reeds, and a hare appears on the path in front of you, staring with large, calm eyes before loping off again into cover. A glimpse of bright blue as a king-fisher flashes from one bank to another. Are those wild orchids, blooming so profusely all along the bank? Yes, they are. There aren't many places left where you can find them in such splendour, but the banks of the Grand Canal is one such oasis.

It has to be said that Ireland's central bogland was not regarded with quite such pleasure by those who supervised the creation of the canal back in the late eighteenth century, since this is notoriously difficult terrain for engineers to deal with. As one such engineer, John Smeaton, commented in a report of 1775:

> Everything that I have seen and done in bog, even in moderate deep sinkings, has been attended with difficulty, and uncertain expenses … Avoid a bog if you can, but by all means possible, the going deep into it.

When the entire centre of the country consisted of exactly such ground, however, it was difficult to avoid the challenge. It was to take decades of exhausting labour, of drainage and clay lining, to ensure the canal would take and continue to hold water. The struggle with bogland goes some way towards explaining how it took so very long to link Dublin to the Shannon – from the height of the canal boom in the mid-eighteenth century almost up to the dawn of the railway age in the early nineteenth.

Still, the Bog of Allen is an intrinsic part of Ireland's history. References are to be found from the most ancient documents right through to the present day in poetry, literature and the many fond reminiscences of those who grew up amid its beauties. Two classic children's writers, Maura Laverty (*The Cottage in the Bog*) and Patricia Lynch (*The Turf Cutter's Donkey*), both immortalised the lifestyle of this world.

Here, skilled men sliced the sods with the sharp two-sided spade known as a sleán, and tossed these heavy wet slabs to children, who 'footed' them in groups of five or six to dry. Once the wind had blown through the sods for a month or so,

Former turfcutting bog being allowed to return to nature.

they were piled on to donkey carts or into creels and carried back to the family cottage, where they were used throughout the year for cooking food and heating the home. Other loads were carried to the edge of the canal for transportation on to Dublin, to feed that city's constant demand for fuel.

Many individual autobiographies too recall the joys of long days spent on the bogs cutting the turf, while mothers carried heavy baskets of food and drink to them in the middle of the day. This way of life is largely gone now, but you can still see the traces of cuttings in the ground levels, showing where families once gathered their winter fuel.

Those who dwelt on the bogland were not slow to take advantage of the new waterway bringing goods and passengers from one side of the country to the other. One of the most endearing examples of local entrepreneurship must be that of Poll the Pishogue.

Mr & Mrs S.C. Hall, who toured Ireland extensively in the early 1840s, met this canny character while travelling on the canal across the Bog of Allen. Poll was a local 'wise woman', who provided cures and charms for the surrounding population from her simple turf hut. When the canal came, she very sensibly expanded her business to include all and sundry who might pass by, especially city travellers eager to break their journey for half an hour or so to experience local colour and tradition.

Poll's company was as mingled as it is possible to imagine; the fly-boat dropped many a passenger within sight of her hut, and the horses were glad to linger in the neighbourhood where their drivers expected some passenger going a few miles

onward after holding consultation with the sibyl of the bog
of Allen. Men going journeys would buy of her 'their luck' – a
defence against the powers of air, fire, water and 'the devil's
books', till their return.

Hall's Ireland, 1840–43

Poll the Pishogue certainly saw the possibilities offered by the
barges passing to and fro, and it is worth noting that this was
evidently appreciated by the operators, who willingly brought
new business to her door, delaying the boat's journey for this
purpose. It is of course entirely likely that they got an extra tip
for so doing.

Just outside Tullamore, heading west, Srah Castle stands
alone in a field to the north. Built in 1588 by an English soldier who married into a local family, it's visible from the tow-

Poll the Pishogue.

Srah Castle on the canalside outside Tullamore.

path. About 3km further along, beyond the twenty-ninth lock, Ballycowan Castle, a fortified house built in 1589, stands on the site of a former castle destroyed by fire. It is itself now a gaunt and eyecatching ruin, resembling greatly the setting for a horror film, although it is within the grounds of a respectably occupied farmhouse, close to the canal bank.

There is a little quayside to be spotted near Kilina, 2km further on, where turf would have been loaded on to barges in days gone by. A large mound in a neighbouring field is reputed to be the burial spot of an ancient chieftain, and it is said that local farmers won't touch it for fear of bad luck. There is a huge old ivy-covered warehouse at the edge of the canal right by the burial mound field too, a reminder that other goods besides turf travelled by the Grand Canal.

About another 2km brings Corcoran's Bridge into view. From here, the ancient churches of Rahan can be explored, a short

Ballycowan Castle.

St Carthage's monastic church and graveyard at Rahan.

stroll to the north. The monastic site at Rahan dates back to the fifth century, and still has two churches standing (one dedicated to St Carthage) and a ruined medieval tower house. There is some beautiful carved stonework here, especially a Romanesque circular window that is thought to be unique in Ireland. Stand in this quiet flat pasture land for a moment and think of the craftsmen who spent so long creating all this beauty, now blown by the soft wind and seen only by incurious cattle.

Becan Bridge, Henesey's Bridge and Ballycloghan Bridge, with the thirtieth lock, come next, not much over 1.5km from Rahan. Cornalour Bridge is by the thirty-first lock, and then we're on a southwest course running, down 3km to Pollagh and Plunkett Bridge. Just before Pollagh, there is an original semicircle still visible, cut out of the northern canal bank, where barges could moor and turn, suggesting that this was one of the many loading points for turf bound for Dublin.

At Pollagh itself, there is a cheerful pub, ideal for a break, and a fascinating sculpture can be found on the canal bank. It depicts a traditional turf cutter or, as it is locally known, The Bogman. Made of 4,000-year-old bog oak, retrieved from the surrounding landscape, the figure stands on a base of local brick, reflecting the fact that there were brickworks here in the eighteenth and nineteenth centuries. The local clay was utilised to make the supplies so much in demand across a country that had building fever.

In fact the construction of the canal, and the ready supply of local clay, could well be said to have created Pollagh. The Irish name, *Pollach*, denotes a land full of pits or holes, which would certainly have been the case anywhere that brickmaking was carried on. Employing many local people, this was hard and dirty work, but nevertheless demanded skill. A busy

The Bogman statue at Pollagh.

brickyard would aim to make 5,000 plus bricks in a single day. The industry lasted up to the 1930s, when the more ready availability of concrete and cement spelt its demise.

St Mary's Church in Pollagh was built of that local yellow brick. The church is noted for both its altar, also built of bog oak, and its stained glass windows from the famous Harry Clarke studios.

Lough Boora Discovery Park, lying just south of Pollagh, was created in an ambitious programme to rehabilitate old turfcutting levels and transform them into a place for exploration and discovery. It's a good place to take children, to help them understand more about the natural life of this environment and to learn what we can do to protect this habitat and all the creatures and plants that still survive here.

Another 2.5km or thereabouts and Turraun is reached. Here a new car-parking facility with pedestrian access to the canal bank has been built, offering a convenient starting or picking-up point for a day's walking or cycling. It also gives access to Turraun Nature Reserve, which, like Lough Boora, has been created on old turf-cutting bogland. There is a lake on this reserve where you can see a variety of waterbirds and waders, like great-crested grebe and jack snipe, as well as plenty of duck. It's a pleasant place for a stroll along the marked tracks, between thickets of gorse with their coconut-scented yellow flowers, and rustling reedbeds, spotting orchids in season, before ending your hike for the day.

Opposite: Turf drying in a bog near Pollagh.

The Bord na Móna swing bridge near Turraun.

Chapter IX

TURRAUN

— TO —

SHANNON HARBOUR

A kilometre or so beyond Turraun is the fascinating Bord Na Móna swivel or swing bridge, built in 1987. This solves the problem of bog railway vs waterway access by incorporating an electrically-operated rack-and-pinion motor that swivels the bridge around to facilitate one or the other method of transport. Presumably either the train or the boat must contact Waterways Ireland to ensure a clear passage is provided. Or perhaps the train has the higher authority?

Still heading southwest, the canal reaches Derry Bridge, and then turns west to cross the Silver River by the Macartney Aqueduct, before heading somewhat northwest again. Bypassing the town of Ferbane, the towpath goes under Gallen Bridge, once an important location for the loading and delivery of goods. The *Dublin Evening Post* of 17 March 1829 carried a notice from Messrs Maher and Adamson

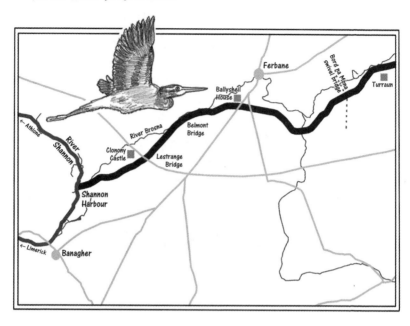

of Grand Canal Harbour in Dublin, stating that they now had lumber and parcel boats plying to and from Dublin and Ballinasloe, with stores at Gallen and Tullamore, 'where careful agents attend to receive and to forward Goods to their respective destinations'. Prospective customers were assured that the boats were new, drawn by two horses each, and that the owners 'retain no person in their establishment but men of tried honesty, sobriety, and diligence'. Comforting if you were entrusting important parcels to their care.

Next come Noggus and Glyn bridges, with a lovely wide grassy route heading towards Belmont Bridge. A nice surprise is presented before reaching that point, though, as the walker and cyclist following the canal are treated to a special view for their eyes only. The waterway is unexpectedly crossed by an old and somewhat crumbling bridge (inaccessible from the towpath below). This leads from an old, disused driveway across to the ruins of a once-stately house on the banks of the River Brosna, a short distance away. This isn't something you could see from the roadside or the window of a passing car. It is reserved for the slower traveller and as such deserves to be savoured. The rooks and jackdaws circle over the chimneys of Ballysheil House, where once noble guests would have congregated, servants rushing hither and thither to do their bidding. Little, however, is actually known of its history, beyond an entertaining note by a schoolboy of the 1930s in the Folklore Commission's records, which suggests that the family of Sheils were wealthy surgeons and more than somewhat autocratic in their ways.

The bridge was in fact built by the Grand Canal Company, presumably at the demand of the mansion's owner, who had no desire to be cut off from his avenue by the incursion of a vulgar modern waterway. It is known locally as Judge's Bridge.

Ballysheil House – what tales could it tell?

Picturesque Belmont and the double Lock 33.

Incidentally, the blackberries are profuse along this section of the canal in late summer and early autumn. Better bring a bag.

Belmont Bridge must surely be one of the prettiest locations on the entire Grand Canal. Beautifully kept, with shining paint and ironwork everywhere, it has a splendid warehouse towering over the thirty-third lock (a double) and quaysides below, showing where grain was brought in and goods shipped out. Look closely at the inner walls of the lock and note the circular indentations there. These were the slots where boatmen would fit their poles to push the barge through to the next gate. Next time you use the phrase 'wouldn't touch it with a barge pole', remember Belmont, where barge poles were indeed used, not only to touch but to propel.

Another pleasant side trip is to walk a little way north of the canal to the five-arched, mid-eighteenth-century bridge over the river Brosna, which here spreads out into a wide and wild

Lestrange Bridge.

display of rocks and sparkling falls. You can stand in one of the alcoves or 'refuges' on the bridge, built to allow pedestrians to shelter from some over-speedy carriage rushing by, and enjoy the view at leisure. A leat cut from further upriver serves the nearby Belmont Mill and re-enters the Brosna at this point. Grinding of grain now having ceased for a century or more, the mill is currently a haven for artists.

It is 2.5km or less to Lestrange Bridge. Here a short stroll north up the R357 brings you to Clonony, situated halfway between the canal and the Brosna, where a tower house built by the Coghlans in the fifteenth century still stands. Later seized by Henry VIII, it was granted to Thomas Boleyn, father of the ill-fated Anne, when Henry began to consider her as his second wife. The tombstone of her nieces, Mary and Ann, lies near the foot of the tower. Very far removed from the plotting and planning of Tudor England this peaceful village and its castle seem today, but in its time, it must have seen much frantic activity, as messengers sped to and fro, bringing letters and information from England's capital to the western reaches of Ireland. The castle is now a national monument and open to the public generally, although with no fixed hours. It still has its own murder hole for those in search of thrills!

Now it's about 1.5km to the thirty-fourth lock, where leisure boats start to appear, chugging gently up and down, or moored along the banks, indicating that the canal is nearing its end. 3km to Griffith Bridge, and at last the final stop, as Shannon Harbour itself spreads out before the traveller. It was October 1803 when the directors of the Grand Canal Company were joyfully able to publish the great news that:

… The line of the Grand Canal has been extended from Tullamore to the River Shannon, near Banagher; and on the 1st day of November next, that branch of the Canal will be opened for general trade and passage boats; and that in order to encourage the traders, the Company will charge no more on that part of the Canal than one half of the toll now payable on the other parts of it, for all goods and merchandise which shall be carried on such extension until the 1st day of May next.

A Passage Boat will leave Tullamore on Tuesday, the 1st day of November next, and every succeeding morning at the hour of four o'clock, and will arrive at Curnalorr (seven miles from Tullamore) at six o'clock, at Gillen at 40 minutes after seven, and at Shannon Harbour at nine o'clock.

The same Boat will return to Tullamore daily, leaving Shannon Harbour at three o'clock in the afternoon, arriving at Gillen at twenty minutes after four, at Carnalorr at six o'clock, and at Tullamore at eight of clock in the evening, from whence the Passengers will have an opportunity of proceeding to Dublin by the early Tullamore Boat as usual.

Saunders' Newsletter, 21 October 1803

The cost of a ticket in the first-class cabin travelling from Tullamore to Shannon Harbour was 5s 5d, with accommodation in the second-class cabin slightly lower at 3s 6d. Unfortunately, though, tickets weren't to be had that October of 1803. Because of leakages, and an exceptionally dry summer in 1803, the official opening had to be delayed until April 1804. By that time, the canal had taken 47 years to build, advancing at a rate of just 7.7 metres per day.

There wasn't actually anything very much at Shannon Harbour when the canal first reached the mighty river, after all those years of effort. It had been decided upon as a practical connecting point, but nothing had been done to prepare the site or build any actual facilities. Plans were quickly made for connecting coaches to the towns of Birr, Nenagh and Limerick; the essential warehouses were soon erected for the storage of goods, and there followed a harbour master's house, several taverns and eventually a large RIC barracks.

Merchants were quick to seize the opportunities offered and advertised their services in the newspapers to let everyone know of this great new water-borne transport system. Thomas Benson was one such:

Thomas Benson informs his Friends and the Public, that the line of navigation being now complete between Dublin and the Shannon, he has established a store (No 5) at Shannon Harbour, for receiving and delivering all goods entrusted to his care, and where he has appointed a steady respectable person to conduct his business, for whose faithful conduct he has received ample security, and to obviate the inconvenience of delay, he has built a house for him to reside in, on the spot.

For the further accommodation of those who are disposed to give him the preference, he has so arranged the business, that his established parcel boats shall ply regularly (loaded or unloaded) from Dublin every Thursday and Sunday mornings, and arrive at Shannon Harbour every Monday and Thursday mornings, will return again to Dublin every Tuesday and Friday mornings with equal expedition. The advantage of such

Once the busiest of waterways: Shannon Harbour and its ruined hotel.

certain and speedy conveyance needs no observation, and the great saving of land carriage by water, being 61½ miles for 25s 8d, or 15½d per cwt (furniture or bulky articles excepted) will speak for itself. Goods for Limerick and adjoining towns sent forward on reasonable terms.

If expedition, regular and personal attention, have any claim on the public, T Benson flatters himself his boats are entitled to a preference.

Griffith Bridge at Shannon Harbour.

NB Complaints addressed to Mr Benson, Tullamore, will be immediately attended to; and he requests those ordering goods, will give directions to have them labelled 'For Benson's Stores', to prevent mistakes.

Dublin Evening Post, 21 December 1805

The magnificent hotel here, like those still standing at Portobello in Dublin and Robertstown in Kildare, was opened to travellers in 1806, and provided a considerable degree of comfort for those select customers who could afford its rooms and meals. That hotel is still quite a sight today. Admittedly it is abandoned and windswept, but it is nevertheless a breathtaking sight, with its graceful frontage and wide steps descending to the quayside, echoing a more stately era of travel.

The Company's Hotel at Shannon Harbour (near Banagher) being finished, the Public are respectfully informed that on the 24th day of June ult, an additional Passage Boat commenced plying between that place and Robertstown, which sets out from Shannon Harbour at Ten o'Clock in the morning, arrives at Tullamore ten minutes before Three in the afternoon, proceeds from thence at Three, and arrives at Robertstown before Ten o'Clock at night; and the Passage Boat which departs from Roberstown at Four o'Clock in the morning, arrives at Tullamore ten minutes before Eleven o'Clock in the forenoon, and leaves Tullamore at Eleven for Shannon Harbour, where it arrives Ten minutes before Four o'Clock in the afternoon.

The Hotel at Shannon Harbour (which the company have let to Mr LUKE HARTON of Banagher) is well furnished and fitted up for the accommodation of Passengers; the prices of Beds the same as at Robertstown Hotel. Post Carriages are also provided by the Proprietor of Shannon Harbour Hotel for the conveyance of passengers travelling from the Hotel.

Dublin Evening Post, 5 July 1806

At the height of its career, just before the railways made their noisy presence felt, Shannon Harbour was a busy place, seeing up to 300,000 tons of produce transhipped annually, and more than 250,000 people passing through. That's a lot of industry for nineteenth-century Ireland. Today it's quieter, of course, but finding a new lease of life, enjoyed not only by private boats and other watercraft, but increasing numbers of keen walkers and cyclists, who make the most of this historic waterway, linking east with west.

The thirty-sixth lock, just beyond the village, is where the canal actually meets the Shannon. Here passengers and goods could be disembarked for onward transport on the river, whether up to Athlone or down to Limerick, by bigger boats, more suitable for journeys on that strong waterway.

And there was once another stretch of canal on the opposite side of the Shannon, leading up to Ballinasloe. It is now almost completely overgrown and difficult to trace, although if you have time and can explore by car, you might find a remaining little stone bridge or two.

Nearly there. The penultimate Lock 35 at Shannon Harbour.

THE FORGOTTEN BALLINASLOE

Back in the early nineteenth century, like so many other towns close to the Shannon, the burghers of Ballinasloe saw considerable advantage in being connected to a major commercial waterway like the Grand Canal and lobbied hard for a branch to be built. They did have the River Suck, but it was unsuited to the boat traffic of the time, varying between wide and narrow, shallow and deep, as well as being very fast-flowing. The Ballinasloe branch was constructed between 1824 and 1828, at a fairly hefty cost of £43,485 (plus an additional eyewatering £2,769 for a wooden bridge across the Shannon). We won't even attempt to compute that in modern currency, but it would certainly be in the upper millions.

Notice is hereby given that on Mon the 29th inst the Extension of the Grand Canal to the town of Ballinasloe in the County of Galway will be opened for trade; and that on and after that day, the Passage Boat which leaves Dublin every afternoon at two o'clock will proceed forward to Ballinasloe, and arrive there shortly after twelve o'clock at noon; and also that on and after that day, a Passage Boat will depart from Ballinasloe at noon, pass the several stages on the Grand Canal THREE QUARTERS OF AN HOUR EARLIER THAN AT PRESENT, and arrive in Dublin at ten minutes after ten o'clock on the following morning.

Mayo Constitution, 22 September 1828

However expensive to build, the Ballinasloe branch served its purpose well for many years, bringing cattle and produce

The remains of the now-filled in Ballinasloe Canal, crossed by the M7 motorway.

down and across for the Dublin trade, and carrying thousands of visitors and animals up to the famous Ballinasloe Fair each year. This October event is one of the oldest in Ireland and was famed throughout Europe certainly since the seventeenth century.

Tradition has it that Napoleon Bonaparte bought a horse here, which he rode to triumph at Austerlitz in 1805. No, we do not know if he came over himself to survey the stock with his characteristically keen eye, but if he did, he would not have had the advantage of the canal, as it hadn't been built yet. Up from France to the Shannon, and then overland by horse to the fair would have been the route in pre-Ballinasloe Canal days.

Closed in 1961, this branch is now almost entirely hidden by the luxuriance of Irish native bushes and trees, relentlessly reaching in to take over anything that isn't guarded constantly, but in its day it would have been a clear route across open country. Indeed, the *Limerick Chronicle* of 21 November 1840 noted of a recent tempest:

> The fly-boat from Ballinasloe was much retarded in its progress on Monday by the storm. The horses which pulled it were twice driven into the canal by the force of the wind between that town and Shannon Harbour.

But – a wooden bridge across the Shannon? Was that even possible? Apparently so. At first, floating structures were used, although the horses drawing the barges were understandably nervous at stepping on to these and required considerable coaxing. A gentleman who published accounts of his travels in the *Liverpool Advertiser* of 1842 noted of his arrival at Shannon Harbour from Limerick:

> This is the point of junction of the Grand Canal to Dublin, and the canal to Ballinasloe, 13 miles from the spot, and at which terminates the steam navigation to the westward. There is here a long and handsome wooden bridge from shore to shore.

A lady who travelled the route from Dublin to Ballinasloe many times in her childhood, going to and from school, was rather nervous of this bridge, always feeling relieved when it had been crossed:

> At Shannon Harbour, we changed into the fly, or fast boat, for conveyance across that noble river, and on to Ballinasloe; and a delightful change it was, notwithstanding the five minutes of terror we endured while one of the horses, which was new to the work, proving restive, and displaying a strong inclination to kick a passage for itself and companions through the frail wooden bridge over which they were passing, and which I conceived to be the sole barrier between us and eternity …
>
> 'A Canal Boat Sketch', *Duffy's Hibernian Sixpenny Magazine*,
> January 1862

Later, winches were used to drag barges across, with horses waiting at the Ballinasloe side to pull the loads on up to the town. The remains of an old iron winch can still be seen on the bank at Shannon Harbour, just where the waters of the

Brosna and the canal come out to meet the powerful drag of the Shannon. If you happen to be coming down that mighty river on a cruise from Athlone, keep an eye out, and you will see a signpost pointing left, marking the entrance to the Grand Canal and the direct route to Dublin. It's nice to see a signpost out there in the midst of fast-flowing waters.

A truly magnificent undertaking and a spectacular commercial waterway. The pity is that the difficulties encountered in the recalcitrant landscape and the many arguments about the best way to proceed delayed it so much that the first whistles of the steam engine were almost to be heard by the time it was completed. (As the Grand Canal finally reached Shannon Harbour in 1804, the first steam engine was being tried out on a line in South Wales.)

Oddly enough though, being overtaken by later technological developments was the saving of the Grand Canal in the end. Being almost forgotten, put to one side, it has survived to become our own great long-distance greenway, linking one side of the country to the other, and providing a never-to-be-forgotten experience for thousands of visitors each year.

We have reached the end of the greenway. Or the start, if you prefer to begin at our greatest river and move east to the capital. Look back at how far you've travelled, or take the first step into adventure. Enjoy every pace, every turn of the pedals, along this great route that stands as testament to the determination and will of those who built it, almost two and a half centuries ago. It is our great heritage.

Journey's End: Where the Grand Canal enters the Shannon.

INDEX

OF

PLACES

A

Abbeylough Bridge 124
Adamstown 59, 64
Allen, Hill of 98
Allenwood 123
Aran islands 84
Ardclough 70, 71
Athlone 182, 188
Aylmer Bridge 68
Athy 18, 29, 86, 91, 93, 95, 106, 113-16, 122

B

Ballinasloe 126, 172, 182-87.
Ballybritan 67
Ballycloghan Bridge 166
Ballycommon Bridge 124, 142
Ballycowan Castle 165
Ballykelly 102, 103
Ballymanus Bridge 113
Ballyshannon Crossroad 106
Ballysheil House 173
Ballyteigue
- bridge 97
- castle 97, 98
Banagher 177, 181, 182
Barrow – river 18, 93, 94,
- Barrow Line Ch V
Becan Bridge 166
Belmont
- Bridge 172, 175
- Mill 176
Blackwood feeder 123
Binn's Bridge 119
Birr 109, 178

Blundell Aqueduct 127
Blundell Castle 130-31
Bogman at Pollagh, The 167
Bog of Allen 17, 18, 126, 139, 159, 162
Boland' Lock 147
Bond Bridge 123
Brosna river 173, 175, 176, 187
Bury Bridge 147

C

Carlow 106
Calverstown 106
Camac Aqueduct 113
Campbell's Bridge 144, 145
Cappyroe Bridge 145
Carlow 106
Cartland Bridge 138
Carnalore 177
Charleville Castle 153
Clane 77
Clonony 176
Clondalkin 17, 53
Cock Bridge *(aka Burgh Bridge)* 84
Colgan's Bridge 137, 138
Coolestown 131
Corcoran's Bridge 165
Cornalour Bridge 166
Courtwood Bridge 112
Corbally 78, 80

D

Daingean *(formerly Philipstown)* 137, 139, 141-42, 148
Derrinturn 124
Derrymullen 123
Devonshire Bridge 72, 73,

Digby Bridge @ 16th lock 82, 83
Digby Bridge @ 25th lock 82, 146
Downshire Bridge 129, 137
Dublin, gen *assim* and Ch I,
- Black Horse Bridge 44
- Bluebell 50
- Canuck river 43, 50
- Christ Church Yard 40
- Grafton St. 86
- Dolphins Barn 32
- Drimnagh Castle 50
- Goldenbridge 45
- Grand Canal Plaza 25
- Grand Canal Street 25
- Griffith Bridge 32, 41, 43, 44, 54
- Hanover Quay 24
- Herbert Place 25
- Inchicore 44,
- Killeen Road 50
- Kilmainham Gaol 44
- Naas Road 49
- Park West 50
- Portobello 18, 20, 28-30, 32, 40, 88, 179
- Rathmines 40
- Ringsend 12, 23, 38, 41, 43
- Rogerson Quay 23
- St Audeon's Church 34, 35
- St James' Church 35
- St James' Gate 17, 18, 32, 34, 41, 109
- St James' Street 38, 43, 50, 72, 88
- Suir Road 32, 37, 41,
- Wilton Terrace 28
Duke's Drain 103

Edenderry Ch VI and 137,
Esker Beg 139

Fenton Bridge 122, 124,
Ferbane 171
Fisherstown Bridge 112
Foranfan 123

G
Gallen *(or Gillen)* Bridge 171, 172
Galway 20
Georges Bridge 137
Gillen 177
Glann, nr Edenderry 132
Glenaree Bridge 98
Glyn Bridge 172
Gollierstown Bridge 61
Grattan Aqueduct 112
Griffith Aqueduct 98
Griffith Bridge 176

H
Hamilton's Bridge 124
Harberton Bridge 123
Hazelhatch 61, 64
Healy's Bridge *(aka Bonynge Bridge)* 85, 86
Henry Bridge 72, 73

J
Judge's Bridge 173

K
Kearneystown Bridge, *see Aylmer Bridge*
Kilbeggan 144
Kilcock 146
Kilcullen 106
Kildare 84, 97, 106, 112, 113, 146, 179
Killeen Golf Club 75
Killeen Bridge 139
Killina 165
Killinthomas Woods 102

L
Landenstown
- bridge 83
- estate 83, 84
Laois 107, 112
Leinster Aqueduct 81, 129
Lestrange Bridge 176
Liffey river 18, 23, 38, 50, 81
Lifting Bridge (Bord na Mona) 124, 139

Limerick 20, 37, 148, 178, 179, 182, 187
Littletown Bridge 96, 123
Lough Boora Discovery Park 168
Loughrea 90
Lowtown 18, 93, 96, 117, 122
Lucan 43, 56, 61, 63
Lyons Estate 68, 77
Lyons Hill 70

M

Macartney Aqueduct 171
Macartney's Bridge 102,103,
Milltown feeder 96, 123
Milltown Bridge 113
Molesworth Bridge 141
Monasterevin 18, 93, 95, 104, 106, 108, 112-13,
Moore Abbey 104
Moore Bridge 107
Mondello Park 84
Morrell river 72, 73
Mount Lucas 139
Mountmellick 107-11. 147

N

Naas77, 78, 80
Nenagh 178
Noggus Bridge172
Nore river 116

O

Offaly 129, 141
- History Centre 147
Oughterard 70

P

Plunkett's Bridge 166
Pollardstown Fen 96, 123
Poll the Pishogue 162-3
Pollagh 166-68
Ponsonby Bridge 72
Portarlington 107, 109, 111
Prosperous 165-66

R

Rathangan 93, 98, 100-103, 129
Rath of Iomghain *at Rathangan* 100

Rathmore Bridge137
Robertstown 17, 28, 67, Chs IV & VI, 179, 182.
Rhode Bridgen 137, 139

S

Sallins 17, 43, 56, 61, 67, 75, 77, 80, 82, 88, 129
Shannon Harbour 18, 20, 28, 64, 88, 90, 93, Ch IX.
Shannon river 9, 34, 80, 91, 94, 177
Shee Bridge 124
Sherlockstown Common 75
Shra Castle 163
Silver river 171
Skew Bridge 96
Slate river 98
Spencer Bridge 100, 102,
Stradbally 106
Suck river 184
Summit Level, The 123
Swivel Bridge, Bord na Mona 171

T

Ticknevin 67
- bridge 124, 145
Tipperstown 73
Toberdaly 139
Trimblestown Bridge 137-39
Tullamore Ch VII & VIII, also 18, 29, 64, 172, 177, 181
Turraun Ch VIII and 171.

U

Umeras
- Bridge 103
- Peatlands Park 103

V

Vicarstown 112, 113

W

Waterford 18, 94, 116, 122
White's Castle, Athy 114, 117
Wicklow 25, 48
Wilson's Bridge 102